THE DISCIPLE

SIMON HAY

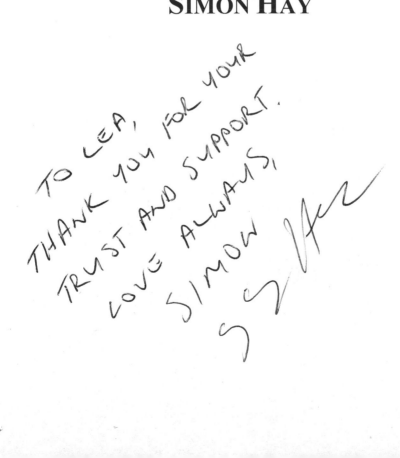

To Lea,
Thank you for your
trust and support.
Love always,
Simon

ISBN: 978-0-9874731-0-3

Printed in the United States of America

Book cover design: Robert Baird
Book layout: Cheryl Perez

Dedication

For Gegu—thank you for having faith in me.

"What has been in the mind of man is in the mind of one." ~ Gegu

THE PRESENT

The story you're about to read is contrary to Christian beliefs. It may be confronting to some readers, but it's not my intention to anger or hurt anyone. The story is true. It changed my life, and is the reason I'm now able to heal illness and injury with physical contact and intention.

For a long time I believed this was to be a story about forgiveness, and then twelve years after this experience, Jesus materialized in my healing room and asked, "Do you know why I chose you?" I did not.

"You were my half-brother and the bravest man I knew. I came because I knew, despite the fear of judgment, that you would stay the course. I came because you were capable of healing me, and you did.

"To everyone else I am the Christ, an ascended master. I'm called on for healing and faith. You knew to heal me. You saw what no one else has. I am a mother's son, not His Son."

This is a healing story.

JUDAS

For most of my life, the only thing I had in common with Jesus was that my father was a carpenter. I was born in a hospital, not a manger, in Tauranga, New Zealand. I wasn't breathing. I'd strangled myself with my umbilical cord. I was a blue baby, not an indigo child or *The Son of a Preacher Man,* and the strangling, not the color of my flesh, is an important fact to remember.

I have one sibling, an older brother, and he also has nothing in common with God's Son. His birth wasn't a virgin birth, and though he was a better swimmer than I, he never walked on water. He swam like *The Man from Atlantis* whereas I swam like a three-legged dog. My brother was seal-pup chubby, which may have contributed to his swimming prowess, and gave me reason to tease him. Sibling rivalry is universal, and I deserved the dead-legs and Chinese-burns my brother dished out.

My brother and I were baptized in the Church of England, and my father said grace before dinner, but we weren't church goers. Nanna, my mum's mother, sang in the church choir, washed and mended second hand clothes for the church fair, but she didn't read bed time stories to us from *The Bible.*

She smelt like freesias and old leather, baked scones, fruit loaf and gingerbread, fed stray cats and played cards with my brother and I when we slept over. Her post-war bath was deeper than the one at home, her spirit generous, and we called on her for homework aide.

I started school in Papua New Guinea as my father was contracted to build a school there, but, other than looking at photos and listening to my father's stories of this time, I remember little. I know that an indigenous couple cleaned, cooked, did yard work, and baby-sat my brother and I, and, even now, I feel loved whenever I think of them.

We returned to New Zealand when I was seven. My mother kept house, cleaned motels, made costumes for me to wear to school parades and volunteered to help on school camps. My dad built houses, renovated our own, played basketball, crewed on a racing yacht, and wherever we went people greeted him by name. This always surprised me and I was proud to be his son.

The best memory I have of my dad is when he woke me in the early morning to watch the FA cup and the All Blacks playing international rugby tests on TV. The worst, when he wasn't there to wake me for anything. He was also a member of the Lions Club, and I enjoyed spending weekends with him doing charity work for the community: building, concreting, fencing, and landscaping.

My mother played guitar and banjo and sang at parties, which were frequent, and she always played records at home. I grew up listening to country music, 50's and 60's rock and roll, 70's pop, and ABBA. ABBA's hit single, *Thank You for the Music,* is an appropriate statement to say to my mother, but by my teens she had abandoned music, and despite having a friend die from cirrhosis, she chose to spend her nights drinking.

My mother also often talked about ghosts. Apparently, they visited while she was house-keeping, and if they were too annoying she'd ask them to leave. My mother was tiny, she shopped for clothes in the teen's section at our local department store, but I never doubted she could command ghosts to disappear. She once rubbed a coin against clusters of warts on my knees, told me she was buying them, and within a week they'd gone.

Mostly, my mother was anxious, not confident, but she always spoke assertively when describing her experiences with ghosts. She unnerved me at times, more than ghosts did, as she always knew where I was and what I was doing. Now, I know she was a gifted psychic, but then, I imagined she was head of a spy network.

From the age of eight years old I spent most weekends and school holidays with my mother's farming brother, and he and my aunty also talked about ghosts. I felt more connected to my uncle's family than my own, and I loved, thanks to my father and pop, working with the earth and animals.

My uncle and aunty moved often, working and living on different farms, and, apparently, a ghost travelled with them. I helped them pack and carry boxes and furniture, but *Casper*, friendly or otherwise, never hopped into the trailer.

My uncle told me the ghost's name was George, and it usually took him a month to find my uncle after he'd moved. We'd be playing cards, doing a jigsaw, or eating a meal, and my uncle would say, "Hello George." My uncle was a joker. He teased me playfully, but I knew, by his relaxed smile and tilted head as if he was listening for a response, that George was real.

George sometimes moved household knick-knacks, turned the electric kettle on and banged the iron door on the wood stove, but he never yelled, "Boo!" Other than feeling observed at times, I don't recall sensing George. My uncle's home always felt peaceful.

Spending time with my uncle was a blessing: he was a father, brother, and mentor, and George was only a small part of that experience. At eleven, I dug post holes and lifted posts other boys my age couldn't roll, and by the time I was twelve I chopped wood and turned over sods of earth all day without tiring. I butchered my first sheep a year later, drove a tractor, used a chainsaw without supervision and cooked a roast dinner using vegetables I'd grown myself.

I also visited a cousin who talked about being woken by ghosts: they appeared at his bedside, sat on the bed and talked to him. I listened when he talked about these incidents, but no one visited when I slept over. I was an Elvis fan and hoped he might appear and sing *Jailhouse Rock*, my favorite

Elvis song, while I was there. I imagined he'd appear with a guitar, float through the door and ask me to sing with him. Instead, I slept soundly and dreamt about the *Green Lantern*, escaping from POW camps, and kissing girls.

I don't recall ever seeing a ghost, but never doubted that my family's ghostly encounters were real. The dark, zombies, and Donny Osmond's teeth frightened me more than the prospect of meeting a ghost. In my father's library was a Reader's Digest book filled with strange stories and amazing facts, which I read regularly. I was interested in the supernatural, but never feared it.

Inevitably, my parents separated in my early teens. My father, due to a knee injury and botched surgery, changed careers. He chose teaching. The two years of adult tuition eroded the financial security he had worked so hard to build. We were destitute. My parents fought, and they both slept with other people. One day it felt like I woke up in a stranger's house. My father was gone, and my mother was an alcoholic.

It hurt, and I buried the pain deep inside. The only time I felt peaceful was when I worked on the farm with my uncle, and I longed to return to his company. Later, after my father had settled into his new career, I visited him during school holidays. He lived in a small, coastal, predominately Maori community, and I grew to love the people and culture as much as he did. His new wife and her family welcomed me as one of their own, and I found a mother's love and a place that felt like home.

My brother and I lived with our mother. Nightly, in the basement of one of the houses we lived in, an angry ghost tossed around stacked cardboard boxes filled with books, dishware, and linen. The poltergeist, content to terrify cardboard boxes, left me alone and didn't mind that my brother and I played pool in his basement.

Eventually, my mother hired a medium to move him on. My brother, present for the house cleansing, later described the floor moving in a wave-like motion while the medium was working. He was wide-eyed; I was hungry, and hoped he hadn't eaten the last slice of ginger bread. Sarcasm and disinterest were now companion states of being when I was home.

I knew my mother had done séances before, but I hadn't participated until I was fifteen. It was a big year: we'd moved again, I'd carried my weight in wild pig down a mountain, dug a grave for a stillborn child and filled it in, reversed my mother's car into a power pole—wounding my pride and the car—played representative rugby, grew kumara plants for sale—earning enough money to buy my own clothes and fix my mum's car—and, with curious detachment, I watched my mother communicate with the dead.

On the few weekends that I was home, our big-breasted neighbor and her girlfriend visited and drank cheap cask wine with my mother. My brother, being older, was often out driving with friends, but we were both at ease with the idea of speaking to spooks. Lit candles and the glow from a red light bulb turned the nicotine stained ceiling into a dawn sky, and Neil Diamond reminded us that *Love Doesn't Live Here Anymore.*

By midnight, squares of paper with letters and numbers on them were arranged alphabetically and in sequence in a circle. Yes and no, written on rectangles of paper, were placed in the center of the circle, and a crystal shot glass was turned upside down inside the circle.

We'd all place a finger on the glass and someone would ask, "Is anyone there?" There was always someone there. The glass moved, hesitantly at first, and then with increasing urgency. The glass, skating across the polished table top, moved from letter to letter and number to number spelling out names, dates of birth and death, and fragmented dialogue.

The guests were always nervous, excited and drunk. I remained calm, refilled wine glasses, and listened to the women vilify cheating husbands and new lovers. I learned that men were bastards and vibrators dependable.

The glass moved effortlessly under the light touch of our pointer fingers, and at times moved so quickly our fingers separated from the glass. I believed ghosts were moving the glass, but I wondered why the glass didn't move on its own. Why did we have to touch the glass?

My mother, the nominated scribe, wrote the letters and numbers down, and often she'd write pages of information faster than the glass could spell them out. Now, after years of working with spirit, I realize she was a gifted trance medium: her posture, demeanor, and style of writing changed with each new visitor.

To place a person in a trance, spirit merges with the energy field of the medium and noticeable changes occur. The consciousness and *form* of spirit manipulate the medium's mind and body to deliver messages, and the medium is transformed into another person.

On these occasions, after the guests had giggled their way home, my mother, exhausted, headed to bed. I'd stay up and passively clear the room of smoke and read, to relax. It's only now that I wonder why spirits—strangers—shared their lives with drinking and smoking divorcees.

Even though I had excellent grades, I chose to leave school early—at sixteen. I was hurting from my parent's separation and lifestyle choices, and grew tired of loaning money to my mother for bread, milk and smokes. The only time I felt peaceful was farming with my uncle, so I completed my last end-of-year exam and two days later I was living and working on a dairy farm.

Six months later my mother reconnected with an ex-lover and moved to Australia with my brother. Before she left she sold everything, including personal items that had sentimental value to me. I felt homeless, betrayed, and it took many years to forgive her for selling my childhood memories. My brother and I barely spoke now. It was difficult to determine why, and I didn't care to ask. I guess we said goodbye at some point, but I have no memory of doing so.

I found it difficult to settle, and changed jobs yearly, moving from dairy to sheep and cattle properties, market gardens and orchards, and lived and worked on scenic properties in the North Island of New Zealand.

I experienced moments of synchronicity: I recognized and knew what strangers were going to say, I often knew what tomorrow would bring, I was an exceptional animal tracker—reading spoor and moving through native forest as smoothly as the animal I was hunting—and I enjoyed telepathic conversations with my farm dog. I knew what my dog was thinking, his thoughts were in my mind, and he knew what I wanted him to do before I spoke or gestured. Daily, my connection with the land and animals grew stronger, but I never replicated the ghostly encounters of my family.

I never thought to share these experiences with any of my co-workers. Farmers talk about the condition and price of livestock, meat and wool, the land and weather. I didn't feel different or isolated, but the longing for something indescribable always haunted me.

At sixteen, the silhouette of a dog and the timing of clouds sliding off the moon saved me from getting shot. I'd gone for a walk with the farm dog, gotten lost, and decided to follow the shoreline to home. A fisherman had mistaken me for a cow and sighted his rifle on me. I spoke to him and his companion, and the shooter said that his finger was on the trigger about to fire, but he paused when he saw the dog in the moonlight. Poaching cattle was common in the area, and if they'd shot me I'd have been tossed into the ocean.

Two months later I slammed into a gatepost while riding a motorbike, was catapulted over a barbed wire fence and landed twenty meters away on a gravel road. The impact winded me, but I stood up without injury.

At seventeen, I rolled a car after losing control on a gravel road—I was the only occupant and no other vehicle was involved—*fell* out of the latched seat belt and regained consciousness sitting on the internal roof of the car. My hands rested on the broken glass shards that spread around me, and I wondered how long I had been sitting in this position. I climbed out of the smashed window and walked the last two hundred meters to home. I woke the next day without a scratch or bruise, and I never experienced any PTSD symptoms from either accident.

At the time, I was working and living on a government sheep and cattle station, and the accident had happened opposite the manger's cottage, early in the morning. Rather than bother him, I walked to the shearing quarters where I resided. I wasn't dead or dying, and the milky way lit the path home. The high altitude and pollution-free atmosphere made it feel like the stars were within reach.

Cowboys work and play hard, and even though I wasn't a cowboy, I always wanted to be. I never contemplated why I was lucky to escape injury: I was young, wild and reckless. Farming toughens you, and life and death decisions are a way of life. Every day was an adventure, and I agree with Bryan Adams, *Those Were the Best Days of my Life.*

I fell in love at eighteen, had a child and mortgage by nineteen, and had separated by twenty-one. The pain I'd buried for so long spilled out of me. People often thought I was older: I looked older, spoke confidently, and was good at everything I did, but the responsibility of being a parent, having debt, and the *sins of my father* betrayed me. We never reconciled, and now my daughter wishes to have no contact with me.

I'd survived poachers and vehicle accidents without a scratch, but love shattered my heart. I *died just a little* and followed my mother, brother, and farming uncle to Australia. I landed with sixty-two dollars in my wallet and a bag of clothes. I'd left everything else with my daughter's mother.

I felt my daughter's and her mother's emotions for three years. I chose not to date for those years. I didn't have a lover but felt it when my ex-partner did. When she was crying, worried, angry, or afraid, I knew, but I never recorded her happiness. I was unaware that I was an empath, that I was able to feel someone else's state of being and actions.

I hid the intense feelings of isolation and heartache from everyone in my life, and I started karate to ease the burden I carried. I punished myself on the dojo floor, and looking back, it feels like I bled every night I trained. One night, I recall doing push-ups and watching a pool of blood from my smashed nose forming on the floor under my face. I loved the brotherhood of sweat and blood and hated myself.

Throughout my life, and while in New Zealand, I had often heard my name called: while felling trees, driving tractors, shepherding, gardening, hunting, in the silence of remote country immersed in nature. Surprised, I had turned towards the person calling me, but there was never anyone there.

I never questioned who the voice belonged to, or doubted that I heard it at all. We drink when we're thirsty, we breathe without thinking about it, and the voice seemed to be a part of me that I never thought about or needed to question.

These incidents stopped when I arrived in Australia. My mind replayed the events leading to my separation, over and over. I was disconnected from my homeland, from my heart, and the rage I'd buried for so long drove me to seek solace in physically exhaustion. There was no love in my life, and the calling voice was silenced.

I took the first available job and worked for a plumber. The job lasted three years; the longest time I'd stayed in any job. I was laid off during a downturn in work, and eventually was hired by a drainage company. Later, after attending night school for six months, I became a drain laying contractor.

Six years after arriving in Australia I did one séance with friends at a party. The glass spelled that my daughter had been assaulted. Knowing felt like being kicked in the sternum. Everyone present was amazed how quick the glass had moved, but were oblivious to how the message had affected me.

I re-connected with my daughter when she was twenty-one years old, met her fiancé, attended her wedding, and said hello to my granddaughter. The differences in lifestyle and the past we shared were too vast to overcome, and our relationship ended again, but before it did, she confirmed the assault had happened.

Except for this one incident, for more than a decade the dead hadn't visited, and it wasn't until Joanne and I dated that experiences with ghosts became frequent again. I first met Joanne when her brother-in-law, Gary, and I worked together for the drainage company. However, it was seven years before we dated.

Gary and I became instant friends. I'm one day older than him. Our personalities were similar, and we both worked hard at work and for family and friends. We often spent time together on the weekends and it was then that my friendship with Joanne grew.

Joanne is energetic, sexy and often times funny. Outside of her family she's bashful, but because I'd spent time socializing with her brother-in-law, I'd seen her relaxed and chatty. Her hazel eyes are playful and penetrating, and she looks you in the eye when she talks to you. She's short, voluptuous, and is handy to have around if you have a fridge to move.

Joanne's, equal parts shy girl and sexy confident woman, and is comfortable shopping with the girls and pouring concrete with the men. Often, she's misunderstood; both men and women are intimidated and intrigued by her strong energy. She's easy to love, but difficult to get close to. I was grateful for her friendship and trust.

It wasn't until I held her hand that I realized we'd never touched before. Considering I'd known her for so long and since I hug my male and female friends the realization astounded me. We'd not hugged, shaken hands, kissed, or bumped into each other in seven years. When we did, I felt like I was home, which is cliché, and a line in a country song, but I felt peaceful for the first time in many years.

I wondered if we both needed to heal from past wounds before we could allow the attraction we'd always felt for each other to become reality. I wasn't conscious of keeping distance between us, but *something* had.

We'd gone to dinner and then to the movies, and it wasn't until we walked out of the theatre that our hands found each other. I sighed and continued to sigh all the way to the car park. We didn't have to learn how to hold hands or to kiss, the timing and the positioning was perfect. We fit together. My heart now ached in a good way.

Joanne and I dated for some months, and then she and her two children moved in with me. Her daughter, Lee, five years old, and her son, Scott, two, visited their father alternate weekends, and it was on one of those weekends, during our courtship, that we had an encounter with spirit unlike any I'd experienced as a child and teen.

Joanne and I were lying on a blanket, talking, when she noticed a light, an orb of *sunlight*, hovering near the ceiling. The light moved when we looked directly at it, and because of the movement it was difficult to focus on. We continued to talk, just enjoying being in love. The light seemed to be responding to our relationship, and we felt comfortable with its presence. The more peaceful we were, the brighter the light seemed.

As time progressed we experienced this phenomenon often. Sometimes, a celestial sphere of rainbow colors or a golden light appeared near or around us. We didn't talk about these events with anyone, and, because the experience felt sacred, we never discussed the reasons why. When apart, we longed to be in each other's arms, but when we were together there wasn't any urgency, and it was this feeling that healed us both from past wounds.

Joanne was interested in spirit, had been to see psychic mediums for readings and believed her grandfather was always with her, but she'd not seen light before. The light intrigued us and we wondered who or what it was.

Now, I believe the lights were a part of our souls. The peaceful feeling we experienced together created a relaxed state and a dual out-of-body experience. The light was us. I've not had this experience with anyone else, or have heard about it happening with another couple. Consciousness, mind, spirit, and souls vibrate at similar frequencies and communicate and co-create constantly. We were witnessing the love we shared dancing around us, and the experience heightened and softened the love we felt for each other.

I worked long hours and Joanne opted to be a stay-at-home mum. As we spent more time together we learned to know where the other was, or had been, without asking. I'd think about phoning home and know she was at her sisters. I'd forget to call to tell her I'd be late home, and she'd call me and ask if I wanted my dinner kept warm or cooked later. Joanne knew if I was driving my work ute, or if I was at the plumbing supplies. I knew if she was shopping, or drinking coffee with her mum.

These moments of connection surprised us both and reaffirmed the love we shared. At times, telepathically, messages passed between us with a glance. At family gatherings we glowed, and others noticed our *silent* conversations and in-sync body language. We were in love, and everyone knew it.

This ability extended to deciphering the moods and the reason for the moods of our immediate families. Joanne and I started to share the same thoughts, and, together, we noticed when something wasn't right with the people around us. It was difficult, however, to channel this knowledge into action.

Sadly, and six months into our relationship, Joanne's father took his own life, and because we had both known something was bothering him, we both felt responsible for some time afterwards. It was more than noticing he wasn't happy, and it may have made no difference, but we regretted not acting on our instincts. In a way, though, his death was the catalyst for this story.

His suicide crushed those left behind. Guilt and rage soured grief, and Joanne, because of the private way she grieved, felt isolated from her family. She was her dad's favorite child, and he had lived with her when no one else would take him in.

He was a heavy drinker, controlling, sometimes violent and had separated from Joanne's mother before we were dating. He always treated me well. We had worked together when I had worked for the drainage company, and we shared similar traits, both good and bad. I burned my frustration and anger up in the dojo, his burned those he loved the most. He was complicated, intense, a loving father, loyal friend: and a bastard.

I thought his actions were cruel, and I was torn between remaining silent and supporting Joanne, and being angry with him and the family for deserting her. The light, extinguished by pain and grief, never appeared during those dark, sad days, but our love endured and the experience matured our relationship.

At the time, Joanne and I were already sharing our home with spirits. We live in a suburb of Brisbane, Australia, in a two-story hardiflex-sheeted house. The house is situated on a quarter acre block, the iconic Aussie dream, and the established gardens are filled with native shrubs and trees.

Often, you can hear footsteps of ghosts, children, running across our wooden floors. As I had lived by myself in this house for some time, I was familiar with these occurrences, but the first time Joanne heard the footsteps we were downstairs talking. Her immediate thought was that our children were running in the house, but our children were not home. I believe the spirit children had chosen this moment to be heard by Joanne; they had been waiting for her.

One month after Joanne's father's death, a falling ornament startled me while I was watching TV in bed. Later the same evening, Joanne went to the toilet and felt someone had accompanied her. Nervously returning to bed, she counted in her head the number of steps someone following needed to take to reach her, and just when she reached the number, a shelf was dislodged from the wall beside her and fell onto the floor. She jumped under the covers, but didn't wake me.

It was impossible for either object to move without the application of considerable force, and though it's not clear how we came to this conclusion, Joanne and I both felt a new spirit resided in our home. The next day I phoned my uncle who had, for some time, been attending a spiritual church. He had met people who communicated with spirits, and I asked if he could arrange for them to come to our home.

I trusted my uncle—he was the reason I came to Australia—and he had remained an influential figure in my life. Through habit, not intention, I spoke to my father infrequently. I avoided everything about my past, disconnecting from friends and family, forgetting birthdays and ignoring Christmas. I hadn't spoken to my mother for many years, as she and her new husband were alcoholics and her selfishness exhausted me. My uncle had always been the light that guided me home.

That evening, my uncle, accompanied by Jesse and his wife Lynda, arrived to help. Jesse's tall, has a truck driver's build and always looks like he's just woken up. His voice is melodious and deep, and I've no doubt he could sing the blues or sell Ceylon tea. When we shake hands, his swallows mine, and he ends every sentence with a rumbling "yeah."

Lynda can stand behind Jesse and not be seen. She's curvy and round: round face, round eyes, round hair, round breasts. Her twinkling eyes make it hard to determine the color, and I assume she uses organic body products because her body odor is strong, but not unpleasant.

Jesse and Lynda are mediums, and together they told us a spirit had caused the objects to fall. The spirit had done this because Joanne's father wished to say goodbye. He had been unable to go to the light without telling Joanne he loved her. He was sorry; he was with his father, and his thoughts were clearer now.

He had planned his death meticulously, but I'm certain he was unaware of the pain he'd leave behind. He'd done what he'd always done: manipulated and controlled. As tough as he acted, I believe he was terrified and tormented on the inside. Bullies usually are. Joanne and I wondered if he was bipolar, and we agreed that he had suffered from depression.

Joanne's father's message eased her grief, and gave her something to share with her sister. They slowly re-established the close relationship they'd previously shared. This moment brought the family together again, and softened the resentment and anger felt by the in-laws. I was able to forgive Joanne's father, which helped Joanne to heal.

It's not divulged who the other spirit is, or why he felt compelled to intervene to help Joanne's father, but over the course of the evening I looked across the room and saw four figures standing together. They seemed to be made of light, a translucent substance like shimmering heat haze from a hot road. I'd often seen movement from the corner of my eye and felt the presence of something or someone, but this was the first time I had seen a complete form.

Inexplicably, I wasn't surprised or alarmed; I looked at the figures for several minutes while Jesse talked to Joanne and then I asked him to confirm if the figures were spirits. Although I was unable to see any facial features, I felt the figures were smiling.

The most potent moment of the evening was a feeling of compassion and peace—the feeling of experiencing something new, something that had gone perfectly. This feeling motivated Joanne and I to attend the spiritual church with my uncle, and it is there that I had the opportunity to join a meditation circle; a group led by Diane, who is a clairvoyant, a medium and a healer.

Diane's energy is disconcerting, and, even when her back is turned, I feel like she's watching me. She's a robust woman, and it's easy to imagine her throwing shot puts or swimming the English Channel. Oddly, when we met, I thought she wasn't wearing underwear. When I looked into her investigating brown eyes, I had the feeling she knew what I was thinking. Nevertheless she greeted me with a warm, cigarette-smoke-smelling hug.

Ideally, a meditation circle leader is a person who has a strong connection with their angelic guides and is able to communicate with spirit. Angelic guides are spirits of a higher energy—not the spirits of deceased loved ones from this lifetime, but spirits who have the knowledge to direct and counsel. Contact with deceased loved ones is often supportive, rather than instructive. In the same way that good football players don't always make good coaches, our friends and relatives in spirit can encourage, but remain armchair sports fans.

Meditation is a doorway and a tool with which to communicate with spirit. Often, the role of the person leading the group is to interpret the visions seen by the meditators. They are assisted in this task by talking to their angelic guides.

Spiritual meditation is like dreaming while being awake. A peaceful atmosphere is created, allowing participants to view and experience past lives, the future, and to have the opportunity to meet and communicate with their guides.

The theory behind meditating in a group is that the combined energy of the group enables each participant to have a more profound experience. The group sits in a circle, and the lights are dimmed—though this is unnecessary. The only benefit is that the clarity, or reception, of the visions is clearer—similar to closing the blinds to remove the glare from a television screen.

Using descriptive dialogue, the person guiding the meditation creates an image in the minds of those meditating, leading to a relaxed or trance-like state, and perhaps an out-of-body experience. People describe floating and looking down on themselves and the group. Some people report seeing random images, while some experience physical sensations: listening to birdsong, the touch of rain, the feeling of walking barefoot. Our spirits are able to experience every sensation of physical life during meditation.

As soon as I sat down to experience my first meditation guided by Diane, I felt smothered and agitated. Once I closed my eyes, I lost control of my body: I couldn't open my eyes, move my limbs, or speak. It felt like a sodden blanket had been draped over me, pinning me to the seat, and water was being poured down my throat. I was unsettled but, surprisingly, not terrified. I wondered if this was what drowning felt like, and then I *popped* out of my body.

I stood in front of my seated body and looked at *The Man in The Mirror*. He looked pale and tense and was shivering. A golden glow behind me caught my attention. I turned away from my distressed body and followed the path that appeared. As I moved closer to a giant tree, backlit by clear night sky, I recorded physical sensations of walking, but in short accelerated bursts. A circle of golden light at the base of the tree drew me forward. The colors of the landscape and fauna that I observed were more vibrant than any I had witnessed previously in my life.

A euphoric feeling, similar to the feeling after an orgasm, coursed through me. I was excited to reach the light, and that thought catapulted me to my goal. Before me was a small pool of water in a raised rock formation. A perfectly shaped lotus flower floated in the pool, and a pair of hands, palms facing upward, rested one either side of the flower.

The hands belonged to an Asian featured man who I immediately knew. He was my guide. His hands were of dark gold flesh, their outline smudged by liquid-like light. Golden vapor radiated from his palms.

The sense of longing I felt when I looked into his eyes was palpable; an overwhelming feeling of recognition, longing and sadness. He smiled and told me to forgive myself. At first, I assumed he was referring to this lifetime, and it took two months of daily meditation to learn otherwise.

His faded burgundy robes glow as if the sun is setting behind him. His eyes look like mini galaxies, the black more vibrant and alive than the sparkling colors in opals. He's solid, with Polynesian curves, and, in an inquisitive fashion, he tilts his bald head to the right.

According to Diane, it's uncommon to have such an intense experience the first time you meditate. For most people it takes weeks, and sometimes months, to see and communicate with spirit.

Once you become adept at meditating with spirit, the things you see are real. You are participating in, observing, and recording the past and future. Locations and experiences are created with exceptional detail. You forget that you're seated, and your mind and *body* become interactive participants in the dream-like worlds you're visiting.

Under Diane's tutelage, I learned to communicate with my guide. I attended weekly meditation nights for two months and visited her during the day when work permitted. Her guiding voice led me to fields, forests, temples, beaches, and other worlds, and my guide accompanied me. I heard his voice, at first only in meditation, and then in my day-to-day life. It was his voice I had heard calling my name in New Zealand.

Now, I sought the voice out. The sound of my name gave me a sense of peace unmatched by any experience in my life thus far. My old farm dog, Tip, used to gently nudge my hand with his nose when I was exhausted or thoughtful. As if programmed to, I'd rub his ears and sigh. I felt loved, and my guide's voice made me feel the same way.

His name is Gegu (pronounced Ged-ju). He's a Buddhist monk and he calls me, "my son". We have shared numerous lifetimes together, and when he didn't reincarnate he has been my guide. There have been times, when I remained in spirit, that I guided him.

In Gegu's lifetime we were twin brothers. It was in this lifetime we developed our strongest spiritual bond. We lived in Southern China, near the Hengduan Shan Mountains, during the 12th Century. Our mother died giving birth to us, and though we are twins, we were not identical. Gegu reminded our father of his late wife. This caused him heartache, so Gegu was placed in a monastery when he was six.

During meditation with Gegu, I relived this lifetime. As a young man I sought comfort by resting outside the monastery walls listening to an anonymous monk play his flute. At the time, I didn't realize I was listening to my brother. Although we spent a lifetime apart, our longing to be reunited persisted.

I tended my father's fields and carted crops to neighboring provinces, married, raised a family, and a feeling similar to the painful ache of separated lovers was always present. That feeling has accompanied me in this lifetime. Within my soul I've searched for an indefinable something. I ache with loneliness.

Tended to by my wife and children, I died of pneumonia and old age. Gegu, sensing my impending death, went into a meditative state and left his body to walk with me into the light. He was able to do this because of the training he had undergone. I later learned that "Gegu" is a title for a teacher, and is awarded when a level of enlightenment is attained.

Under Diane's direction and Gegu's guidance, I re-visited past lives during meditation. In every lifetime I was a warrior. I fought for Khans, Emperors, Kings, and tribal Chieftains in every country and period of time. I have led men into battle and to safety, after generals and warlords had fallen. I have guided caravans of refugees from danger, and walked away from, or lost, my families and lovers to war. Loyalty, service, brotherhood, loss and betrayal were common themes. I killed men. I was good at it.

I developed a sense of *knowing*; similar to having a sixth sense: to intuit the future, to be aware without evidence. Personally, I believe a sixth sense is the result of our five senses working in harmony, and we can sense further and in a spectrum broader than human consciousness records. A blind man still sees, but not how we perceive sight. He intuits his surroundings. Now, after years of communicating with Gegu, I can sense environments around people I'm thinking about, no matter where in the world they are.

Mothers are *wired* to recognize their baby's cries, and respond to or ignore those cries accordingly, yet mothers cannot describe how they are able to do this, only that they can. Mother and child are connected even when they're apart. The mother vibrates at; *I will care for you*, the child at; *I need care*. This creates the pathway for the mother to *know*. They share the same mind; one mind. Language and description separate mind, body, and spirit, but they are not separate entities.

A sense of *knowing* is a state of mind, a pathway of communication, or a level of awareness developed with meditation. I *know* Gegu is smiling without the processes of being aware. I don't need to see him; I don't need to believe he exists—he is smiling.

During past life meditations I am repeatedly reliving the same life. Diane felt that I had been Mark, one of the disciples of Jesus. My mind emptied. I felt disconnected when she said it, and I knew immediately that she was wrong. The clothing I was seeing during meditation matched those from this period, but it was difficult for me to accept and process rationally the thought that I may have been a disciple.

Away from Diane, during meditation at home, I visited bearded old men and wise men with shepherd's crooks and staffs. Seated on worn rocks, they spoke with passion in a language that was foreign and familiar: one in particular watched me intently. His long, flowing beard always moved as if blown by winds, and later I learned, from Gegu, the movement was caused by the energy radiating from him.

The field of consciousness is in a state of flux. Simultaneously, energy and information flows in infinite and multiple directions. Recorded through human consciousness, the flow appears to create movement. The elder appeared to move because he's recorded in a liquid-like stream of information. It's the same effect as if you tried to remain still while suspended in an ocean current.

We never spoke, but simply sat together observing the surrounding landscape—a desert of sorts; dry and rocky with occasional grasses. This man appeared frequently, and it was always the same: I'd walk towards this seated elder and crouch in front of him, which always seemed to amuse him. On occasion, he'd put his hand on my shoulder and stare into my eyes. When he finally spoke, he introduced himself as Elijah and addressed me as "the betrayer." I'd once been thrown from a horse (in this life), and it took forever to hit the ground: Elijah's words had the same affect; time slowed. An invisible hand squeezed my heart. I exhaled slowly and wondered if I'd ever breathe again. After this introduction, he stood and walked away. I waited for the pain, but I only felt confused and sad.

At home, I meditated nightly and visited the meeting place of the debating men, where, after a few weeks, Moses appeared. With a spark of recognition I moved to greet him, and we embraced like old friends. Holding my shoulders firmly, he stared into my eyes and grinned.

We sat and talked, a mentor and his student, separated from the other men, but afterwards I could never remember what we talked about. Gegu advised me that what Moses shared with me was information about how to work with spirit, but I'm unable to recall this knowledge because it has been assimilated into my spirit for future use.

One Christmas, when I was a child, my father bought me an adventure children's bible and Moses was in it, but not this Moses. The art in the bible was great, but my favorite books were *The Adventures of Marco Polo*, *The Famous Five*, *Nancy Drew*, and *Commando* war comics. To have recognized Moses and to have had a conversation with him is, for me, like believing that aliens are coming to dinner.

My nightly meditations continued, and I spent my evenings not only with biblical figures, but also with shamans and witch doctors, chieftains and kings, knights and barbarians, and spirits of children, and they all called me, "the betrayer". The title felt comfortable, as if it was the name I'd always had. Then, Jesus arrived and called me Judas. From that moment my subsequent meditations were spent with Jesus and his family.

Surprisingly, my meeting with Jesus wasn't as emotional or as intense as my first meeting with Gegu. Jesus greeted me warmly, and we embraced. I felt in love, as if we'd been lovers, and his scent and presence comforted me. The pain came later, after I'd remembered the life we shared.

With Jesus present, the clarity of the meditations increased tenfold; the glow of previous meditations softened, and the scenery was as solid as the landscape in my physical life. Meditating with Diane, I believed I had seen Jesus in some of the meditations, but we had not spoken. Now, I was not only seeing Jesus in my meditations, he was also appearing in my physical life.

I continued to work long hours, and Jesus sat cross-legged on the ground and talked to me while I measured, cut, and glued PVC pipes together. We conversed in my mind about his and my life. He was curious about everyday things: the household bills, Lee and Scott's welfare, and he turned his head and looked at the excavator operator, building supervisor, and plumbing inspector when they spoke to me.

On the weekends, when I cooked breakfast for Joanne, Jesus was the most visible. Smiling, he sat at the table hoping to be served. I'd have thought he'd be happier visiting the Pope, but no, he enjoyed the meals at my place. I turned water into tea, and he was happy with that.

Often, we met and talked on the shore of the Sea of Galilee. The water was crystal clear and much colder than I expected. My body was seated meditating, but *I* was walking in water. The atmosphere was hazy, the air dry, and I was surprised by the wetlands that encroached into the surrounding hills. I'd expected a dryer terrain. Jesus watched me curiously as I again became familiar with our homeland. I accepted this was real, and I never felt the need to research ancient Israel.

Now, his greeting was, "my brother," or "old friend," and during these meditations I became Judas—in both physical form and personality. Noticeably, my body odor changed; I smelt like Judas, and in my real life I walked through Jesus' spirit, and at times he felt solid.

In one meditation, I experienced crucifixion—Jesus and I became one—and, looking through his eyes, I endured the moment of his death. I looked into the Roman soldier's eyes when he delivered the final thrust. I felt the weight and pressure of the blow, and my relaxed meditating body shuddered violently. My eyes snapped open. I could see the short spear, and I tumbled off the couch. Frantic, I grasped the shaft of the spear. It felt rough, warm and sticky, but within seconds it disappeared.

I'm sure Jesus chose to share that moment with me to experience the release of his spirit from his battered body—the peaceful tranquility of being free, and the relief of returning to his Father. The violence and pain, though shocking, was softened by the blissful feeling of connectedness to an indefinable *something*. I was aware; not of anything in particular, simply aware beyond feeling.

Of all the lifetimes one may wish to have lived, who would choose the one of Judas, the betrayer of the Son of God? It was a difficult realization. To the Christian world the name Judas is synonymous with betrayal, but Jesus treats Judas like a brother and has forgiven him. It has been difficult to forgive myself, though. My connection with Jesus in this lifetime had opened a vault within me, and mine and Judas' pain and guilt tumbled out. It felt like Ridley Scott's *Alien* tore a hole in my chest, and I had moments of almost unbearable sadness.

The burden of this knowledge drove me to exhaust myself over the coming months. My body became the anvil that Jesus and his family used to give voice to their lives—hammering on my soul with the often pain-filled memories they wanted to share.

I stayed up past midnight night after night transcribing this story, and I continued to work twelve hour days, often six days per week. My muscles ached, I struggled to lift my legs, and it became difficult to fall asleep.

Diane and Gegu had one more skill to teach me before I could accomplish what Jesus had asked of me—to let a spirit use my body to speak, to become a trance medium.

The first time I did this, Diane guided me through a meditation. The old recliner I slumped into was too low to be comfortable and smelt of body odor. Diane sat opposite. She was wearing underwear; her thin cotton dress clung to her curvaceous thighs, and the candles on the coffee table between us burned brightly.

In the meditation, I was sitting on a log in a clearing talking to Gegu. A man walked into the clearing, greeted us, and positioned himself behind me—the *me* sitting in the chair meditating.

It's difficult to comprehend, but I'm able to see into and out of the meditation. When a spirit enters my body I'm able to look through his or her eyes and see the scenes that he or she is describing: a moment in their lifetime, or a memory of their lifetime. It's like going to the movies and becoming one of the actors, and being able to watch the movie and the audience simultaneously.

Gegu looks after my spirit, and we communicate while my body is being used. Gegu also controls the spirits who wish to use my body. He is the bouncer for my *nightclub* and keeps the patrons under control. I've since met people who see spirit clearly, and while I've been in trance they have seen me in spirit.

During trance the spirit uses my body and my voice, sifting through my mind for words and phrases, searching my dictionary and thesaurus. My posture and tone of voice changes, and I adopt the gestures of the visiting spirit.

Though I am aware of what is happening I often don't remember what I have said until people who witnessed the trance talk about it. During the trances in this book, I had no idea what I'd said until I played the recordings back. The emotion is overpowering. Every emotion I feel is amplified, and the people around me usually associate with, or react to, the emotion more than the words I am speaking.

When I transcribe the recording, the spirit from the trance stands beside me and gives me more information. The room *dissolves*, and I'm in the story. It is always easier the second time I communicate with a spirit. I can hear them clearly, and also see a *movie* of the event.

Not everyone trances this way. My uncle, the farmer, is aware of nothing while he's trancing. He experiences only the feeling of the spirit entering and leaving his body. He doesn't remember or feel any emotion, or know who has used his body to speak.

I believe that everyone is able to communicate with spirit, but in an individual way. I can't explain how I'm able to trance. I can only share the experience. Witnesses have described seeing the outline and detail of the speaking spirit superimposed over my seated body. Jesus' face has replaced my own, and turned to look at the people present.

JESUS' BIRTH AND THE JOURNEY HOME

After falling asleep to the sound of rain and waking periodically to look at the clock, I turn the alarm off before the glowing red numbers flick to 3 AM. Walking past the open window, the hairs on my arm are teased erect by the cool breeze pushing through the insect screen, and a green frog sweetens the morning with his song.

The bathroom light is too bright for my eyes, and I'm reminded to shut the door by the sleepy growl of an ever-vigilant mother. "You'll wake the kids." The shower fills the bathroom with steam, and as the hot water massages my back, Gegu says, "Good morning." I smile. I'm alive.

Usually, mornings preceded another painful day of boredom and repetition, working to an impossible schedule to make someone else happy, but not today. It's October 31, 2000, and this is the day I will start the Jesus story with my friend, Narelle.

Narelle and I met at spiritual church, and later she joined the meditation circle with Diane. Our friendship grew, and we started to meet socially for coffee. Narelle's in her sixties, the top of her head barely reaches my chin; she has delicate, warm hands, an enquiring mind, and a school teacher's demeanor: authoritative, educated, and world-wise.

Previously, Narelle had lived in the UK, and she has friends who are clairvoyants and mediums. She's a Sai Baba follower, and a portrait of him hangs in her country décor cottage. The first time I entered her home, the portrait seemed to come alive, and Sai Baba's head turned and followed my movements.

Narelle is guarded around Diane, and doesn't believe Diane is as developed spiritually as Diane thinks. This battle of egos is too common amongst spiritualists, and I theorized in this case it was fuelled by jealousy, as both women believed I was their own special project. What intrigues me, however, is that both Diane and Narelle believe I had been a disciple of Jesus.

Narelle has told me, the first time we met, she knew I had been Judas— I had his eyes. This was a strange moment, and looking into Narelle's grey eyes I could see she was sincere. I'd not shared my meditations with her at this time and wondered how she could be so certain. Later, she told me spirit had directed her to come to Australia and find me. She had been meditating for many years and had seen Judas in her meditations.

Driving through the rain to Narelle's, Jesus joins me, and together we pray. Before this, prayer was a foreign practice for me. As a child I said goodnight to stuffed toys and a cat, and didn't kneel to praise God. Now, I pray to be a clear channel for his words; I pray for truth, and I pray for strength and commitment.

Jesus squeezes my shoulder. He has farmer's hands: confident, dry and calloused, like stressed leather. His hand is warm, and the contact ripples through my body causing me to sigh. I'm a child again; excited to be going away camping for the first time.

Jesus has a soft vibration, gentle and caressing, and he fills me with peace and well-being. Momentarily, I see through his eyes, then I blink and the moment passes. The feeling of his beard lingers on my jaw line, and my hand reaches to remove the hair I think I now have there.

Vibration is the word used to describe a spirit's energy: a unique frequency, an imprint of contact, a trail of passage, the means to determine the source of received knowledge.

If we think of God, or the Universe, as being a pool of water of infinite dimensions, and individual spirits as drops of water falling into this pool, the disturbance of the water by each drop is unique—it has its own vibration.

When spirits come close, we feel their vibration as shivers: light tingling or goose bumps of varying intensity. Every living cell, molecule, thought, emotion, action, inanimate object, and spirit has a singular vibration. Vibration is a soulful frequency and the language of the Universe.

As I drive cautiously through the rain, Jesus chats and watches the road pass by. I watch him from the corner of my eye. I've learned not to turn to look directly at him, as I'm unable to see him this way—he fades away, in time with my turning head, like an elusive fish darting across sunlight-reflecting waves.

Sometimes, he is a shy man, saying little but smiling often, and other times he is animated and charismatic. His eyes are gentle, childlike and calm. At times, they are deep wells of sadness, while in other moments they radiate warmth. The blue is ever changing, which softens his high cheekbones and chiseled face. His hair is dusty blonde, sun-lightened brown, and his beard is thin like an adolescent's. He has a tanned complexion, and is built like a middle-distance runner—lean, with good muscle definition, and of moderate height.

I arrive at Narelle's, and after coffee I prepare to trance while Narelle turns the computer on. We're both nervous with expectation, our hearts competing with the Formula One racing car whine of the hard drive. The air in the room feels heavy and smells like burnt dust. Narelle is worried she won't type quickly enough to record what I'm saying, but she has worried needlessly, because Jesus speaks slowly, and in time with her typing. While I'm speaking, Narelle sees the scenes of the story in her mind, and experiences all of the emotions.

During the trance, Jesus greets Narelle as Grandmother, as her spirit had lived the life of Anna, mother of Mary, in his lifetime. This revelation surprised me and was the reason spirit had brought us together. It also validated the experiences Narelle had during her meditations in the UK. Narelle tells me afterwards, that while Jesus was speaking, she remembers Anna's memories.

Unexpectedly, after Jesus finished talking, Joseph also used me to speak. This was the first of many trances where, as one spirit left my body, another entered. Throughout, the conversations of spirit have been transcribed word for word as I spoke them.

Jesus

"Hello Grandmother. We had been travelling with a group of merchants when we settled for the night, four hours travel from Bethlehem. My mother's waters had broken shortly before midday, and when we set up camp for the night, my mother's labor was well advanced.

"Among the camel merchants was an experienced midwife, Grandmother Beth, and her presence was one of the wonders of my Father, the Great Provider.

"Our cover for the night was a three-sided awning-like tent, with one side open to the fire for light and warmth. Grandmother Beth supported Mary's head and shoulders while you, Grandmother, watched for my arrival. Although her labor pains were not severe, it was an arduous birth for Mary, because she was frail from the journey.

"I remember the cool night air against my flesh as I came into this world, and it is you, Grandmother, who helped pull me clear. You bit through the umbilical cord and released me.

"The feeling I remember the most was the sense of relief and contentment of those who watched over me, and I don't know how quickly other babies see, but, Grandmother, your face was clear to me.

"There were no shepherds at my birth, only two young goat herders attracted to the fire and the sound of our voices, and when you bathed me in warm water then raised me to your shoulder, I saw one of their faces in the firelight. He would later become a thief, and hang with me on a cross.

"This is one of my gifts; to have a knowing of my people, to sense the nature of their hearts, and even as a newborn I was able to do this.

"Joseph was not present for my birth. Directed away by you, he was at the fire with wine and bread—which he had traded his carpentry skills for in Bethlehem—supping with those who traded by camel.

"These are the wise men of which your history books have written; simple traders of cloth and spices who traded goods at the frequent auctions held by the Magdalene's.

"There was no inn or stable. I was birthed in the land of my Father's choosing.

"Mary's milk was low, and she passed into a restless sleep, so you warmed some goat's milk and by dipping a soft cloth you were able to rest my cries.

"Joseph didn't ask after Mary, because he was weak with wine and the company of the serving girl at the traders' fire.

"In this world, after the comfort of Mother Mary, it is your heartbeat I hear first, Grandmother. You did not sleep this night, cradling me while Grandmother Beth tended the fire and watched over Mother Mary.

"I'm aware of the swirling emotions eddying around me as I drifted off to sleep, and when I closed my eyes, I slept in a golden glow, not in darkness. As I grew older, this glow remained ever present, my constant bedside companion.

"My father Joseph will speak now. Please do not judge him harshly."

Sitting with Gegu, I observed Grandmother Beth preparing a broth made from cannabis and honey for Mother Mary to sip, and after the birth she massaged olive oil into her breasts. Mary had given birth in a crouched position, and the smell of birthing fluid, carried on the condensate rising from baby Jesus, reminded me of my own children's birth.

Jesus was born on a Tuesday, two minutes to midnight on the twenty-fourth of March. He was laid in a goatskin-lined wooden box bought from the two young goat herders. After the birth, Beth brewed a herbal mixture for Mary to sip in order to restart her contractions, and it took another two hours before Mary's womb gave up the afterbirth.

When Jesus is describing being fed with goat's milk, I'm conscious of Grandmother Beth's hands warming the milk in a bronze bowl over a small fire, and I react to the warmth, surprised by how cool the night air is.

I'm already aware of Joseph, as Jesus had turned to look at him while using my body. The light from his fire is highlighting his strong cheeks and catching his eyes; shadows lay across him, but I am aware of his full tangled beard and thick, wavy hair. Sighing, Jesus leaves, and joins my spirit as Joseph enters my body. Joseph's torso is broad and square, his forearms are thick and powerful, and his legs, disproportionate to the rest of his body, are lean.

Jesus and my spirit sit together beneath a nightscape of stars in the country of his birth and watch his father speak. His shoulder leans against mine, and I'm comforted by the contact. His body odor is pleasant, and reminds me of sandalwood scented massage oil, and I move my leg so I can also feel his thigh against mine.

Joseph

"Hello, Anna. You and I have had many battles, and my shame is heavy. You cast me away from my son's birth, so I sat with the men and drank the wine I had labored for, but I could not shield myself from the temptation of the young girl who served us. Her father was a poor drinker, and I waited for him and the others to sleep.

"I led the young girl away from the firelight, and while sweet Mary was giving birth to Jesus, I pushed her fresh body to the rocky ground and lay upon her. She mouthed no protest when I lifted her robe and forced myself into her. We disturbed no one, and by morning, I thought of her not.

"When we woke the next morning, my guilt and impatience demanded that we travel, and I had no heed of my son or Mary. We argued, Anna, but you held fast, and so we waited two days for Mary to gain her strength before we travelled, while Grandmother Beth stayed to help you mind the child.

"When, finally, I looked upon my son and gazed into his strange blue eyes, I knew he could see what I had done, and sense my guilt. I did not know how this was possible, but he stirred my stomach to nausea.

"His eyes are like the deepest oceans, swirling and ever-changing, but always clear, and ever since that day, I am cautious meeting his eye, because I know he can see into my heart.

"When we began our journey home, Mary was laid in a low cart drawn by a donkey, and there was another to carry my tools and our baggage.

"We passed many people on the way home, and traded news. This is how news travelled in our land, and it is because of this that history has been wrongly written. Your books are full of hearsay and second telling.

"We carried with us the sense that Jesus was different, and sure enough, when we stopped at one of the wells to quench our thirst, the first of many strange events occurred.

"A father and his young son filling their gourds distracted me, and when I greeted them, the air was suddenly filled with a strange new sound. It was not unpleasant—a soft, musical hum.

"I looked upon the father and son, and their faces radiated wonder. I turned towards Mary and Jesus, and around them were many colored butterflies and golden light. The butterflies were not of the desert, and I had never before seen such colors.

"We spoke not of this incident as we continued our journey, for the wonder had left us fearful to talk of it.

"I will leave you now. Thank you for listening to me."

Joseph's embarrassment and shame is a weight on my chest and it's uncomfortable trancing him. At first, he is hesitant to talk about this incident, and I experience his indecision, but Jesus prompts him to speak.

When I become Joseph, I feel his lust for the young girl. My breathing is shallow, and I steal glances at her full buttocks moving under her robes when she walked. Joseph is charismatic, and has an aura of masculinity to which the young girl responded. Self-consciously, she is encouraging Joseph by touching him whenever she serves him, and is tempting him with her eyes. Culturally, it's easy for Joseph to manipulate the girl. She has been raised to serve her elders, and her father has commanded her to serve the guests at his fire.

When trancing, I not only narrate, but also participate and feel everything, physically and emotionally. I feel the cool night air, the warmth of the girl's flesh, the ache caused by the discovery of the wet down on her mons, taste the peppery scent of her breath, and smell the smoke from the fire on her robe.

I experience fragments of emotion of all the participants in the story. I'm Joseph, but I'm also the girl. She enjoys defying her father, taking risks, and seducing men. I'm looking out of Joseph's eyes, but when *I* blink, I'm the girl. Her age and maturity surprises me, but, because I've been connected to Joseph, I know that thirteen is past marrying age.

During the trance the part of my personality that would judge Joseph for having sex with, in my eyes, a child, is switched off. I'm a participant and an impartial observer. I'm not myself.

Joseph didn't feel any shame until he woke the next morning. By *becoming* Joseph, I realize that his actions were not intended to hurt Mary or his family. He was able to have sex with the girl, so he did, which is how he lived his life—passionately, arrogantly, and without thinking about the consequences.

The following morning, November 1, 2000, I am once again up at 3 AM. On the way to the bathroom I check on Lee and Scott. Lee is snoring, and Scott is lying across his bed; his uncovered feet hang over the side. Joanne doesn't stir when I untangle myself from her warm embrace. The feeling of her warm breasts against my bare chest linger. She's excited for me, but chooses to be excluded from the process of trancing with spirit.

Mary talks to me while I'm showering. She is happy I'm writing about her son's life. Her velvety voice is soothing, and she has an engaging manner of speech. Smiling, she's telling me she is taller than she appears.

She's petite, and looks like a girl I fell in love with in Primary School. She has long black hair, commanding hazel eyes, and, from a distance, she looks like a teenager. Up close, the small lines around her eyes and the occasional sadness reflected from them, makes you realize she is a mature woman. None of the paintings of the Madonna have captured the strength and authority of her features. Her face is long, not round, her posture proud, not demure. She has a scar on the web of flesh between her right thumb and index finger, and a habit of rubbing it with her opposite thumb when her hands are clasped together.

She smells like … I want to say roses, but she shows me a small, white and yellow, star-shaped desert flower, which is picked with stems and leaves, pulped, steamed, then pressed and added to filtered olive oil, warmed in the sun and then filtered again. The end product is kept cool, and used like a body lotion.

Her scent keeps me from moving, and, strangely, my eyes, looking back at me from the bathroom mirror, captivate me. There's something moving in the earthy hues, and longing courses through me. I slowly close my eyes, and Mary encourages me to dress.

"It's time."

Jesus accompanies me again while driving to Narelle's. We talk about the rain and he cautions me about my driving. Universal consciousness enables him to understand the modern world I live in. He *exists* in my world by linking with my consciousness, and I *enter* his world via his. It's a partnership of mind and no-mind, physical and non-physical. The wind is ferocious, and heavy rain lashes the windscreen. Intermittently, he turns to look at me, and his smile is infectious. Although I'm tired, I am looking forward to trancing with him again.

Jesus

"On the journey home, we frequently passed travelers, and I was able to sense the mood, both somber and joyful, of these often weary people. Disturbed by these shifting moods, and beyond the protection of Mary's womb, I travelled poorly.

"Mary was weak on the journey home, and it was you, Grandmother, who tended to her. You had the wisdom to let me journey against her breast, and it was during that time that I learned of her life. I was only a few days old, and yet I was able to scroll through her memories of her life to that point.

"You and Joachim were both loving parents, but Joachim was often away travelling, and Mary felt lost during her father's absences. Your bond with Mother Mary was strong, and she inherited your soft heart, which I know she has passed on to me.

"It was a relief for us all when we neared home, as there had been tension between you and Joseph on the journey. He had been sullen and tense, and had no time for Ruth when she rushed out to greet us.

"She was only four years old, and tried to take me from you, but you held her at bay. Ruth persisted, until finally you let her hold me, but you made her sit on the ground. When I looked up at her, I knew she could hear the sound I was hearing—the singing voices we heard at the well.

"Zebedee's wife, Miriam, was fussing over the struggling Mary, and after you had all moved Mary out of the sun and onto the cot inside the kitchen, you prepared bread and soup for the family.

"Miriam sat with Mary for the remainder of the day, and helped her to bathe and brush her hair. She always had an endearing way about her, and a warm and gentle touch. If she had been born a man, she'd have been one of the twelve disciples."

The aroma of Anna's cooking reminded me of my stepmother's bacon-bone and puha (sow thistle: a staple green vegetable of the Maori people) boil up. A warm contentment flowed through me. The scent and feeling returned when I listened to this recording.

"When you returned to Ruth, who was nursing me, a small bird, a kind you have never seen before, was perched on her toe. It surprised you that the bird had stayed, despite Ruth's chatter, and this reminded you of the butterflies at the well.

"I am three years old now, and Ruth is the angel who keeps me from under your feet. Joseph is often away working at his trade, so you and my mother are my greatest comfort, and together you raise me.

"My mother has less time for me now, for James had been born in the spring, and Jude is on the way. Grandmother, we both know that Mother Mary is pregnant before she knows it herself; It is a secret we share.

"It's common that I sleep with you at night, comforted by your warmth and secure in your arms. One night, we are woken by a strange light shining through the window above our cot, but we do not feel afraid, only curious, and at peace. A beautiful woman materializes from the light. She speaks to us, and says we are being watched—by her and others like her—and talks about many miracles to come.

"I'm three years and eight months old, and using small sentences to talk, but I do not need to speak to communicate with this angel—I can hear her in my mind."

During the trance with Jesus, I had experienced what it was like to be the baby Jesus. Lying against Mary's breast, his spirit was able to feel her weariness and access her memories. Even though he hadn't yet learned a language, and the only physical memory he had was the comfort of Mary's womb, his spirit was able to process and absorb the emotions and the states of health of Mary and the passing travelers.

From this experience, I believe the physical body of baby Jesus is a vessel for God. While writing this last sentence my mind stopped at, "is a vessel for …", and it was Gegu who said, "God." But he also communicated, "As are you, my son."

Perhaps the souls of all newborns record information this way?

It was an unusual trance, because while Jesus talked about his baby memories I felt physically helpless and dependent on Mary and Anna, but I also experienced an adult level of awareness and reasoning. Physically, I felt like a newborn, but intellectually, I felt like an adult.

Mary

"My older sister, Miriam, welcomed us home with her sons, James and John, and her daughter, Hannah, who is three years older than my Ruth.

"Neighbors, drawn by the excitement of our return, wanted to see baby Jesus, and in what is commonly your way, brisk and bossy, you told them not to fuss over the child, but it was obvious you were glowing with pride.

"Before the baby Jesus, it had only been Ruth who could soften your sternness, and after much fanfare, you let her hold the child.

"At times, I wonder whether I am a good mother. We shared so many chores, and with Miriam's boys coming over, and Zebedee wanting to get them out to sea as soon as possible, there were always too many mouths to feed.

"I don't remember much of Jesus' birth, but I do remember the enormous contentment I felt when he was in my arms. I'd like to think we shared his upbringing equally, but he did favor his time with you.

"Compared with the other children, it took a while before he was walking, although other things interested him. He was often found talking to himself, but he was a happy child who always brought out the best in people.

"He was closer to Ruth than he was to the boys. She used to drag him around in an old blanket, and it seemed that every time they returned indoors they had a flower or a pretty stone, a butterfly or a lizard. Together, they discovered little treasures the rest of us overlooked.

"Jesus found beauty everywhere, and he shared this gift with everyone. The only one he didn't seem to affect was his uncle, Zebedee, who only had time for fishing, and his Miriam, whom he kept constantly pregnant.

"Joseph was a man of shifting moods, either ecstatic or surly, and when he was surly it was usually because he was burdened with guilt from his frequent infidelities. Our family and community knew, but we forgave him this failing. Joseph worked hard and was a good provider, and we shared a fondness in our own private way, but it was hard to find the time to be intimate, because we had a large family that made constant demands on our time.

"Of course, you never missed out when Father came home, and to our delight he often embarrassed you. Those moments made us laugh, because you were always so refined, and he could fluster you so.

"Jesus loved his grandfather, but was often reserved around him, maybe a little jealous, I think, of losing your attention to him. I knew Jesus was special, but many of his miracles were shared with you."

Mary's candidness is a surprise. Strangers have always shared personal information with me. It seems Mary trusted me.

This was the last morning Narelle and I worked together. She fatigued quickly and declined to continue waking so early. I'd been directed by spirit to trance with Jesus and his family early in the morning, but I don't believe the time of day had any significance. I viewed the request as a test of my resolve.

"Will you do this, my son?"

"Yes."

"Are you sure?"

"Yes."

We shall see. We'll ask him to wake up at 3 AM, and if he does, then we will know he's the one.

I decided to record the trances with a note-taker, and share the material with Narelle, but four weeks later, she withdrew her support. She was disturbed by the graphic content of the trances, and believed I had been taken over by a dark force. For much of her life Narelle was a practicing Catholic. She has had extensive bible study in her lifetime, and it's difficult for her to ignore what she has been taught to believe.

She became distant, suspicious, and, noticeably, avoided speaking to me. Later, I learned that she'd contacted friends in the UK to discuss what she believed, that I was being influenced by dark entities. She believed many of the stories in the bible to be true, yet had walked away from Catholicism for new age spirituality, a belief system that was supposed to be, in her eyes, a gentle angelic path to enlightenment. She believed Jesus and his family were ascended masters, enlightened divine beings, and not regular folk with real lives.

By this stage I'm like an addict looking for his next fix. I'm committed to Jesus and his family, and being in an altered state reliving someone else's life feels normal. The midwife, Grandmother Beth, uses my body at home.

Grandmother Beth walks leaning forward as if she's in a hurry to get somewhere or is about to wrestle a sumo. When she walks, she stabs the earth with a gnarly walking stick, and her hands remind me of Albrecht

Durer's painting, *The Praying Hands*. Her face is weathered and wise, and her nose is as sharp as her wit.

"You're a cheeky young man."

I'm glad she likes me. She's looking up at me, and I'm not sure if I should bow or step aside. I opt to smile, and she flashes stained and crooked teeth. Grandmother Beth charges through life with purpose and verve, and she is compassionate, caring and stubbornly loyal.

This is how she remembered Jesus' birth.

Beth

"I was travelling to Capernaum to stay with my brother, Itharus, when I first met Anna and Mary. I liked Anna straight off—a straight talker who never stopped fussing over others, and Mary was a pretty young thing.

"Mary's waters had broken at midday, and Anna's party was already settled when I happened along. Of course, I offered to assist: what a way to start a friendship! It wasn't a particularly difficult birth, but Mary was fatigued from her journey. She was awfully thin, and it was clear the baby would be struggling to get a meal from those small breasts.

"Anna and I worked well together, delivering the baby boy in the early hours of the morning. Little Jesus came into the world as they all do, squawking and bloody, and some young boys gave us goat's milk for the child, because Mary's milk was slow to come.

"Bloody Joseph was nowhere to be seen, drinking and carrying on with the traders. I disliked him on first sight. Late in the night, I needed to pass water, and as I moved away from the firelight for privacy, I was disturbed by his grunting as he had his way with the young daughter of one of the traders. I could see him in the starlight, humping the poor thing.

"She was too stupid to say no, and Joseph was too much of a pig not to try to seduce her. The little tramp was enjoying it, and I was unmoved by her whimpering. How could I say anything to Anna? She was too concerned with her Mary.

"In the morning, Anna argued with Joseph, telling him that we must stay in camp, which tested his patience. I had no time for him at all.

"Before the traders left, I cornered the young girl whom Joseph had seduced. I gave her some herbal powder to take, in case she was carrying a bastard. She asked after the baby, and I almost slapped her smart mouth.

"The mother and boy travelled well. Mary slept a lot, which was good, while my friendship with Anna grew. The boy drew us together, for I knew this boy; I had seen him in my visions.

"I remember the wadi. I didn't see the light, but I heard the voices. Yes, young man, that is what I heard. I was not surprised. I didn't talk about this with Anna, as it had unsettled everyone, but I believe it had happened in order to heal Mary. She travelled easier after this, and when next I bathed her, I could feel that her vagina had healed under the soft cloth.

"Arriving at Anna's home, I rested and ate with her, taking my leave the next day for Capernaum to sit with my brother, for the family needed to settle the baby. There were many hands to help, and I was taken with the warmth in the family, but I loathed Joseph, and ignored him whenever I could. I promised Anna I'd return in a week and reside with her, for it was only my brother I wished to see in Capernaum.

"I believe God's hand was in Jesus' birth, and I believe God led me to Anna and this boy. I was not fond of my family, only my jolly Itharus, and we spoke about this Jesus. We knew he was an angel from God.

"When I returned to Nazareth, Anna was pleased for my company. I had herbs and teas made from desert plants, and these helped Mary to regain her strength, and brought on her milk. Goodness, prior to that, I don't know how she could have fed a mouse, let alone a boy.

"I stayed in Anna's home for nine months, until it was Joseph who forced me to leave. I could no longer stand his moods, or his lusting."

Beth's dislike of Joseph is a challenging feeling to trance. She hates him. Jesus is disappointed in his father's behavior; Beth is judgmental. The contrast in views is the reason Beth has spoken. Jesus wants us to view his life from different perspectives. There's also an element of healing in every story. The energy of Jesus' life is present in collective consciousness. Aspects of our lives are similar to Jesus', and that's the point: Jesus was a man, not *Jesus*.

THE DISCIPLE JOHN

Max is a good friend, and he's also my boss. He's a plumber, and I sub-contract to him. In Jesus' lifetime, Max was the disciple John—Zebedee and Miriam's (Mother Mary's sister) son.

Max trains with me at karate: he's balanced, strong, and loves a scrap. He's a bloke's bloke, built like an NRL forward, drinks over-proof rum, and his thick hair has turned prematurely grey. Gegu told me he was John, and after Max had meditated with me, his guide confirmed it.

Max was raised a Jehovah's Witness, and has, at times, struggled with the concept of spirit. As a child he was able to see spirit clearly, and saw his guide many times in the mirror. This frightened him. He was unable to talk about those encounters with his parents and suppressed this gift.

Now, at age thirty-four, this gift has been reactivated. As he moves through his life, he sees spirit everywhere as colorful shapes of energy, and is able to recognize individual spirits by their vibration.

Max underestimates his ability to communicate with spirit, and doesn't realize that often, when he speaks, it's not *him* talking, but spirit speaking through him. Max's main guide's name is Janu, a Chinese advisor and bodyguard to an Emperor. In Janu's lifetime, Max was like a son to him. Janu's enemies killed his wife and child, and after Max saved Janu's life, Janu adopted him.

After trancing with Narelle, I called in for coffee with Max and Janu. I told Max what had come through in trance, and then we started talking about Mary. Gegu and Janu joined the conversation and answered our questions.

Mary's birth date is the sixteenth of November. She was a virgin when she married Joseph at age fourteen, while he was thirty-six. At age fifteen, she gave birth to Ruth, who was fathered by Lazarus Magdalene. My partner, Joanne, had lived the life of Mary's daughter Ruth.

This was the only time Mary was unfaithful. She was young, and had been hurt by Joseph's womanizing, while Lazarus was vulnerable after the death of his wife, who was also named Ruth. Max and I had been told this previously, but at first we struggled to believe it. We live in a Christian world, and it's not until belief systems are challenged that you're aware of how ingrained they are in your psyche.

At sixteen years of age, Mary gave birth to Rachael, but because of Mary's poor health, Mary's sister, Miriam, raised her. At age eighteen, on the twenty-fourth of March, Mary gave birth to Jesus. At age twenty-one, she gave birth to James, and at age twenty-two, she gave birth to Jude.

Miriam's husband, Zebedee, was fifteen years older than Miriam. Together, they raised six boys and three girls of their own, as well as raising Rachael. Two of the boys, John and James, had been fathered by Joseph, and would later become disciples.

Max was John in this lifetime, and though he claims not to remember, Gegu and I recognize that Max is using John's memories during these conversations. At times, using peripheral vision, Max looks like John.

I'm aware that the name Mary is the English translation for Miriam, so does this mean Mary's sister's name is also Mary? I suspect not, but I've not being given another.

Nazareth was not where it is shown on maps today. It was a broad community, rather than a contained township, and extended to the shore of the Sea of Galilee, which was a larger body of water than it is now, and supported a more diverse variety of life. Also, the river Jordan had a greater volume, and flowed more vigorously than it does now.

There is an outcrop in the region of Nazareth that has a view of both the Sea of Galilee and the Mediterranean Sea, and from this vantage point, in the right light, the two Seas appear to become one. This became a safe meeting place for Jesus and his followers, and it was here that Jesus' body was taken for burial.

The landward side of the outcrop forms an amphitheater. Jesus' body was laid in a naturally formed chamber in the center of this three-quarter moon-shaped formation. A slab of rock, natural and unmarked, sealed his crypt. A product that looks like tree sap was used to waterproof the chamber. Jesus' cadaver was moved four years later.

Jesus and his followers travelled in small groups, and used obscure and varied trails to reach this elevated haven. The families and homesteads in the surrounding lowlands acted as sentries, and children, runners, warned of danger. Two memories are always present: we travelled with caution and often at night, and women joined our discussions and enjoyed equal status.

While Max and I are talking, Gegu and Janu are helping us to see the answers. I believe that what I see is from Judas' memories and I'm thankful for Max's friendship and, by association, Janu's knowledge.

Often, before we have finished asking the question, either Max or I have the answers in our minds: I think about asking Max, "Is the story about Jesus' resurrection true." And before I have spoken, Max said, "Jesus's body was on the cross for five days. I wonder who wrote the story about the tomb and the rock that was used to seal the entrance?"

"I don't know, but Gegu has just said three men took Jesus' body off the cross at night. One of those men was Joseph of Arimathea."

Janu often visits me at home. His duty is to Max and to God, but his wisdom and presence can be anywhere it's needed.

Using the word God irks me; it's too masculine, and because it's a name, I feel it categorizes an ideal. New-age disciples might prefer the expression *the Universe*, or *Higher Power*, but that makes me think of something that can be measured, or at least described.

Our body doesn't contain our spirit; tentacles of light radiate from us, an infinite spaghetti of energy fibers of *something*. We're all connected to each other, and to the earth. This invisible field transmits and receives information more efficiently than Bill Gates' empire. Theories of evolution and religion can be debated and recorded, accurately or inaccurately, but this *something* remains an impartial, mysterious observer.

That observer is consciousness beyond the form of consciousness; a source of potentiality and possibility. Human consciousness—the art of mindful and mindless investigation—creates that which we are seeking: the answer to the question, "what is it?" By asking, we are creating what we seek.

Our minds can hear the conversations of the field, but only pertaining to our existence within it. The energy fibers of *something* transmit, record, and store the vibrations of human and earthly existence. The *something* stores the answers for questions not asked yet, it is life not yet created, a state of no time and all time, a database of everything before this moment and everything to come.

What information was in the field before human existence? I've searched for the evolution of man during meditation. I cannot find our starting point. I believe we created God; *He* didn't create us. If I'm right, where did we come from?

Without the function of human consciousness, my descriptions and investigations are meaningless and valueless. The *something* is the absence of human and universal influence. Nothing.

MARY AND LAZARUS

Mary joins me while I am typing. Sighing, she tilts her head to the side and leans against me. My daughter, Lee, interrupts me, and Mary whispers, "She's beautiful." Lee has eyes like saucers, and my arm moves, automatically programmed to embrace all children within a radius of one meter. I turn and look into Lee's anything-I-ask-for-you-are-going-to-give-me eyes. Heaven help me—yes, yes, yes, to all questions. Mary smiles.

Lee wants ice-cream with Milo sprinkled on top, and she'd like me to dish it for her. Mary waits patiently. I walk through her shimmering silhouette when I carry the bowl of ice-cream into Lee's room. It feels like walking through a cool breeze. The first time I walked through spirit, I threw my arms up to push the person away and fell forward. Panicking, I flailed my arms around as if I had walked through a spider web.

When I return and sit in front of the monitor, Mary's long hair lays across my face, and, in a feminine gesture, I brush it aside. When I glance at the computer screen I'm looking through her eyes, and her lashes distract me. I raise my hand to wipe my eyes, because it feels the same as having a piece of lint caught in your eyelash that is obstructing your vision. I'm used to only looking past my own lashes.

Mary is here because I've been thinking about her. I had, with Gegu's help, realized Mary is as gifted as her son, Jesus. If history has branded Jesus the Son of God, then Mary, I feel, must be God's Sister—with a capital S.

For her to have had an affair with Lazarus, she had to have been driven by a stronger emotion than lust, but what? Mary has come to answer that question.

Mary

"Hello, Simon. I have been worried about you. I've been watching you, and I had hoped that you would speak to me sooner. I know what it is you seek from me, for you and I have had more than one life together.

"When Archangel David first appeared to me, I was a child. He came to me in my dreams, and lifted me gracefully into his lap. He embraced me, shielded me with his love, and said unto me, "You have been chosen, sweet child, to be the mother of the Son of God. He will need a compassionate mother and a strong father."

"'You shall call the son Jesus, and he will do many wondrous things. He will lean on you, for he shall lack strength, so we must find him a father of great power, a father with the confidence to stand before men and speak. The man that you seek will be called Joseph. He will be older than you, and he will hurt you, but you must rise above this for the sake of the Son, and for the sake of the Father."

"And so David connects us, Simon, and you have been a part of this plan that has taken so long, and yet is nothing, for two thousand years is merely one breath.

"When I married Joseph I was fourteen years old, and although I pretended, it was not a happy day for me. I watched the man I was to marry drinking with and coveting my sister. I was innocent, but I was not so naive that I didn't know what had transpired between them.

"The first night lying with my husband, I endured him upon me, but for all his faults he is a good provider, and we were married only a few weeks when he travelled once again to ply his trade. It was not my place to judge. My role was to love—which I did.

"Only once in my life did I stray: and it was beautiful. I was attracted to an old family friend, a man I had served before my marriage when he sat with my father. He had lost someone dear to him, his beautiful wife, and how he pined. It was such a night when he came to our home, heavy with his agony and grief. After we had eaten together and everyone had retired, I sat up with him and talked soothingly.

"I asked him to talk about Ruth. He described his loss, and I was attracted to him, drawn to his love, and his tenderness, and then I was in his arms, or perhaps he was in mine. It was beautiful, gentle and wondrous.

"In my moment of deceit, my mind was clear, and I gloried in the love of the Father, and David watched over us so the darkness could not creep in.

"For an hour of love, I lay with Lazarus, with this magnificent man whose heart belonged to another, but for a time, I made him forget. There had always been beauty between us, and it was not a foul thing, it was a wondrous thing, blessed and protected by David, and this is how gentle Ruth came to be.

"After that night, I lay only with Joseph, to show my family love and support, and after his drinking and his rages, when I had calmed him with my flesh, I talked to David and thought about another night with a loving man.

"I knew my son would die in his thirty-fourth year. I knew many things about my son. I knew all the secrets of my family that have been shared with you. The burden of this is the sadness I carry."

Mary's eyes betray her calm speech; they glisten with unshed tears, and I bite the inside of my lip while she's speaking. *I* look up, as if I'm looking at the doorway in Mary's home, and I'm waiting for Jesus to come home. He did not.

"Yes, Simon, I knew Judas. The man distanced himself from everyone, and liked not to bring attention upon himself. He was cautious with trust, and yet had so much faith and love for beautiful Jesus. He could not warm easily to people, so people did not warm easily to him."

I see Mary's memory of Judas: my head is lowered, I've turned away from her as if I can't look at her, but Mary knows I'm aware of everything. She walks towards me and reaches for my hand. I'm terrified of her touch, and I flinch. Gently, she holds my hand between hers, and, with thumb and pointer finger, traces the mass of raised scars that cover my hands. She loves me! I feel like vomiting.

"One time, I approached this young man and, looking into his eyes, I told him, "I know what you must do and I know how it will be done, but do not forsake your own life as my son's path is already set. Believe in what you feel in your heart, not what you wish to see with your eyes. Have faith in my son, and faith shall be yours." Alas, it was not to be for Judas.

"You betrayed him for what? What you had been shown as a child. Not compassion, not love, but only the value of silver. Your father was a drunk and a gambler, and he taught you nothing, and so he betrayed you.

"The power you had been seeking from Jesus was already inside you. Your pieces of silver slipped to the ground and in your last breath, as you slipped from your body, David embraced you and took you home.

"How does a mother hide her pain from the rest of the world? How does a mother watch her son die? How does a mother walk among the people he had come to save?"

Mary's light was bright, and she was gracefully gentle with me. Her sadness, a light kiss, and the ache of responsibility she carried for God was her delicate touch on my shoulder.

Mary's script is startling, and I was unaware that I'd spoken this way until I played the tape. My childhood was an adventure: war games, fossicking for rocks, stamp collecting, bush walking and sport. And my dreams were filled with the sound of *Steve Austin's* bionics and running in slow motion. Angels and Jesus were absent, and my only super power was my ability to interest old ladies and dogs.

The words, "God's Son," "His Father," and "can I watch Benny Hinn?" are as foreign to my lips as chanting with the barmy army. It's my voice, but the words are peculiar to me.

The writers of the bible have used the story of the virgin birth to create separation and subservience. The real Mary is like all women: she became pregnant by having sex with a man. Together men and women create life. *We* are God, but, singularly, women nurture new life and give birth. Mothers are powerful. Jesus lived his life because of a mother's grace, not God's.

Mary's not angelic; she's divine because she's an intelligent, beautiful, passionate woman. Jesus' gift of intuition and healing were activated because he was carried in a womb and loved by a mother. Mary was an exceptional medium, clairvoyant and angel communicator.

If the founders of Christianity had been women, there'd be less violence and hatred in the world. The vibrations of sacrifice and guilt wouldn't be in human consciousness, and passion would be expressed, not repressed.

MIRIAM AND MY KITCHEN

On the morning of November 2, 2000, I arrive home from Max's after our coffee, and while Joanne uses the computer I do the dishes. It's been raining for three days now, and the ground is too waterlogged to lay drains. I'm not used to not working and I'm restless. Standing in front of the sink, and through the condensation forming on the windowpane, I watch a leaf blown by the wind. The leaf lands on the pergola roof before being flung into the grey abyss.

In our kitchen a feeling of awareness and peace manifests at the kitchen sink, and a golden ray comes through the window. When Max visits, he can see it; I can feel it, and spirits will often get my attention there. Like a choreographed advertisement for a sparkling clean and streak-free wash, angels shine, *as bright as bright can be.*

The window frames rattle, and Miriam, Mother Mary's sister, materializes beside me. My left side tingles and I shiver and sigh. Her hands are clasped together in front of her, her head is down, and she's biting her lip. Her skin is the color of golden syrup and flawless. Even though her head is lowered, she's still taller than me. Her plain hemp robe doesn't hide her alert breasts and made-for-spooning hips.

While I juggle cooking breakfast and washing dishes, she asks if she can speak to me. Her body odor is seductive and my hips change shape when she steps closer to me. I'm becoming her.

Gegu directs me to find my note-taker and record Miriam's conversation. I clip the note-taker to my collar and continue with my chores. Miriam moves close to me again. Momentarily, I feel dizzy and bewildered. I lean against the sink and watch the rain lashing the lawn. I glance at my reflection in the window and see two faces—Miriam's and mine. Joanne, used to my antics, smiles and leaves me to it. I've no idea who was cooking breakfast while I was talking to Miriam, but somehow my body seemed to manage.

With Gegu's help, I am shown everything we speak about; sometimes through Miriam's eyes, and sometimes as a bystander. I'm also able to talk to Gegu, and he lets me know how Miriam is coping and what I should say.

Gegu is solemn. "Miriam will share something she has never shared. She trusts you. Jesus trusts you."

I cough to clear my throat and say, "Hello Miriam, how are you?"

"I'm a little nervous."

"I can understand that."

"No one ever knew."

Gegu cautions me to be gentle, and shows me the images of her story. I see and feel everything when I answer as Miriam.

She is crying now. We are crying now. She hesitates again.

"I was so young, you know. I was only nineteen."

"It's okay, Miriam. Take your time."

"I'm so ashamed. I don't even know how it started. Joseph always appeared to be so strong. He was a handsome man, and he had this way about him. You knew he was teasing you, you knew he was …"

"I knew he was teasing me, but somehow, I let him get away with it. He was an elder, you know. It just sort of happened … we had been drinking."

Gegu is one step ahead, and he is already showing me how it happened.

"It's alright, Miriam. I'm not judging you. I've learned many things since working with spirit, and I think you're brave for coming to see me. I'm crying Miriam, but it's okay. You can lean against me."

When she touches me, I am smothered by the weight of her guilt. I haven't time to think how this is possible. Now, I'm completely unaware of my surroundings, and, surprisingly, I'm Miriam and myself at the same time. My throat is tight with emotion, my lip is quivering and it's difficult to speak.

"It was in the corner of the courtyard where the stables were. We didn't even lie down. It happened so quickly, and I felt out of control.

"The secrecy—it was the only thing in my life that I did not have to share. I've always seemed to have to answer to someone.

"The hardest thing was that it would have hurt Mary if she had found out—and then I fell pregnant, and I knew it was his. Zebedee was excited, because we had been trying for another baby for a while. We already had two boys, Luke and Michael, named after the brother I had lost, and young Hannah.

"Whenever Joseph returned home from his preaching, or from his trade, we would go down to the beach behind the rocks. It wasn't really that good. It's just that it was so tempting. The excitement—I think we met about a dozen times.

"After James, I fell pregnant with John, who I believed was also Joseph's child. That was the last time I let it happen.

"I'm feeling better now. By listening, you have eased my burden. I do not feel it in the place we go, but when I come close to this earth …when I come close to this place, I am aware of it again."

Miriam is using the analogy, come close to this earth, to inform that spirit only feel pain communicating to the living. Generations of pain remain in human consciousness, here on earth. It's up to the living to live peacefully, to forgive, to be compassionate—to love. Miriam told her story to heal the *living* Miriam.

"Thank you for coming, Miriam."

"Thank you for asking."

"It's okay, Miriam. Wipe your eyes. We have all made mistakes. Have a look inside my heart, and you'll see some of mine."

"Thank you, Simon."

Later, after playing the tape back, I realized *I* had been speaking. It's unusual for me to trance this way, and this was the first time that *I* had spoken while trancing. Also, I'm normally seated and not moving around. I have no recollection of cooking breakfast, and I was surprised to be standing in front of two plates of farmer's choice breakfast—sausages, eggs on toast, and fried tomatoes—when I opened my eyes.

What Miriam hadn't said, but I had seen, was the first time she had sex with Joseph. It happened during the seven days of celebration for Joseph and Mary's wedding. The insatiable and almost violent sex she'd had with Joseph was incompatible with her gracefulness. Miriam's shame and guilt were genuine.

After Miriam has left, Joanne and I eat breakfast. Joanne smiles as I try to explain what I have just experienced, but I'm still feeling Miriam's emotions, and when I talk about her I need to cry. It's hard to chew sausages and eggs with a trembling lip.

Joanne's main guide—whose name coincidently is also Miriam—and Gegu are standing together watching us. They look amused. I imagine because Joanne is laughing.

While Joanne and I are talking, a ray of golden light encircles us. This is from Gegu—a sign of his love and service, and because it has encircled both of us, he is showing me that he serves us both.

During breakfast I also notice another spirit waiting patiently. I turn to Gegu and he introduces me to Joachim, the Grandfather of Jesus. Joachim and I have tranced before at Narelle's. He had enjoyed flirting with Narelle, which had made her blush. He reminds me of the shorter of the *Two Ronnies*. He's a comedian with a permanent cheeky grin, and I can't look at him and not smile.

After breakfast, Joachim and I wander downstairs to trance. He smiles as he watches me set up the note taker.

Joachim

"Simon, it seems that you know all the secrets of my family now. Miriam is lighter after speaking to you. While we are in spirit, we are at peace, and busy working for the Father, but when we come close to the Earth, yes, you are right: you are able to ease our pain.

"My Miriam was fourteen years old when she met Joseph for the first time. This was at her wedding to Zebedee. Rumors followed Joseph, but I am the kind of man to dismiss rumors, for my faith is strong—I believed in the teachings of Abraham.

"For want of a better description, Joseph is a three-dimensional man: a man of faith, a man of trade, and a man of deceit. Mary would not leave him, because she believed in the vows of marriage.

"I know what had transpired between Joseph and Miriam. You only had to look at the two boys to know they were not Zebedee's. Zebedee must have known in his heart, but he was a hard-working, God-fearing man. He had strong beliefs and a stronger love for Miriam, who shouldered her guilt well.

"She seldom kept a secret from us, and so it must have been a huge burden for her, as she was gentle and loving with everyone. Everyone in Nazareth knew her, and welcomed her smile. She was a tall woman, which was unusual in our family. She was striking and had beautiful hands.

"When they returned with young Jesus, I was not at home. I was away in Assyria trading silks and spices. This was a consignment of the Magdalene's. Working with the Magdalene's, and many other merchants, kept me from my family.

"I love my Anna and my children, and the loss of Michael (at sea) was a great blow to our family. Although there were many tears, this loss bonded us, but it affected Zebedee greatly, and he built a fortress around himself. He became sterner and less patient, and drove his boys harder at work. He was a perfectionist, who loved the sea, but it had taken someone dear to us all, and I think it affected Zebedee more than anyone.

"He spent two days floating in the ocean, and I don't know what he clung to, other than to life. It took him three months to recover. His face was badly blistered, and the scars never fully healed.

"He was already hardened by the weather, but the hardness was now in his eyes. Only Miriam could soften him, and only my Anna could make him laugh. To the rest of us, he was a sphinx.

"Nazareth is a large community with many small homes located along the shore, and only a few set back more than three hundred meters from the beach. A small marketplace trades daily, and a lot of people moved through Nazareth from the inland sea.

"Fishing fleets provide food and industry. Ferrymen transport people and make trade possible, providing an easier and more comfortable journey to Capernaum, a staging point for exporters and importers.

"You are making me smile, young man. There are other towns I wish to speak of, and in time, I will be able to—in the future.

"You have the gift of emotion, and you call all of us to you. The Father is watching your work, and the funny man is happy, and, yes, proud."

This is a comfortable trance, Joachim's easy to work with and he found it amusing that I was unable to pronounce the names of many of the villages he wished to mention. My biggest stumbling block is that I'm aware of where Nazareth is marked on a map, and so I feel the pressure of challenging history. I believe this fear prevents me from saying out loud the names of the townships Joachim wishes to talk about.

It's out of respect for my reader and my sense of responsibility to spirit that I bare my soul for dissection—the soul of my thoughts. Gegu is observing me write. If I'm honest, he honors me, spirit honors me; I honor myself—*a few good men*. Although I'm not aware of what I'm saying I am *listening* to what Joachim is saying. I am the conversation and all parts of the story: participant, observer, and the observed.

Spirit is pulling the word Nazareth from my mind. The phrase, "the community of Nazareth" may mean a Nazarene, or a Galilean from the province of Galilee. But what I'm certain of is that Jesus' family did not live where Nazareth is shown on historical or present-day maps.

While Joachim talked about travelling and trade, I observe that the main trade out of the Nazareth community is fish treated in salt brine or dried. Occasionally, sardine-like fish are cured and pickled in large clay pots with thick walls. These are insulated with papyrus or locally grown flax, that is weaved together to conform to the shape of the pots. Flax growing and harvesting is a profitable industry, and flax is used for many things: oil, wicks, binding, and cloth.

A criticism I have received is, if I'm trancing Jesus, why am I not speaking in Aramaic? Well, I don't speak Aramaic. Spirit trawls my mind for words, for memories of events, and for emotions that can be used to present stories. Spirit improvises and edits the information to construct the conversation. Many years after these events, while in trance, I spoke in another language, but I don't know what made it possible.

When I trance with spirit, Gegu injects me with truth serum. The signed prescription is for unlimited repeats—by God, doctor of medicine and everything else—but it's arrogance for anyone channeling messages from spirit to suggest that the dialogue is not influenced by the vessel used for this process: our minds and physical bodies.

In my physical life I also have difficulty with names. I knew Joanne for seven years before we dated. I was good friends with her brother-in-law, and I noticed that Joanne's family (and only her family) called her Ed. No matter how many times I heard her name, or asked, I could never remember if it was Joanne, Joan, Jo, or Jane, and so I became the only person outside of the family to also call her Ed.

This trait also interferes when working with spirit. All the names in this manuscript are spelled how they sound to me and, therefore, I confess, they may be spelled incorrectly. For me, the most profound experience of trancing is connecting with the emotion, and becoming the *character*.

If I had a university degree in history or languages, or if I had been an academic, the stories Jesus and his family share would be political or academic, and I wouldn't have any trouble with names and their correct pronunciation and spelling; but I'm the "clay" spirit has to work with and, to quote Jimmy Barnes, *"I'm a working-class man."*

The more time I spent with Jesus and his family, the quicker I developed spiritually. I began to see spirits in the flesh: not just in my mind. The landscapes and characters I saw in meditation were materializing in my physical life.

Walking outside one evening, I see a family of North American Indians setting up their tepee. They look up and acknowledge me with a smile. Feeling foolish, I wave back. Standing in line waiting in a bank, I look up when I hear my name called and I can see the spirit guides of every person in the room. They have all turned to look at me.

These occurrences are brief, only lasting a few seconds—unlike what happened when Jesus visited me in my kitchen. One morning, while doing the washing up, I felt the all-too-familiar tingling across my shoulders, and Gegu whispered, "They are coming."

"Who? Who is coming?"

"The children."

My kitchen window and wall dissolve, and I'm standing in a valley blanketed with tufts of grass and wildflowers. The surrounding hills are crisscrossed with tracks, pathways made by animals winding their way between the scattered rocks, and intermittent groups of trees.

Like a trail of ants, a caravan of robed children enters the valley. The older children carry the younger ones on their shoulders, while others lead donkeys hitched to carts laden with fresh foods and baggage. Chickens and ducks are in wooden cages stacked alongside suckling pigs and sacks of potatoes.

Young shepherds herd nanny goats and horned sheep, accompanied by laughter, singing, and the clinking of pots and pans as the wagons travel towards me. The older boys start to pitch camp while the younger children play, fussed over by girls in flowing white dresses.

All the children greet me by name when they run past. Lambs brush up against my legs, and a ball bounces nearby, a laughing boy in hot pursuit.

It is then that I notice Jesus walking towards me through the children. His arms are outstretched, and his hands brush against the children as if he is walking through long grass. Butterflies and pollen float in the golden air around him.

A child leans against me, and I can smell the scent of the wildflowers that carpet the ground. As Jesus comes closer, I can see he is holding a young boy's hand, but when Jesus reaches me and embraces me, the boy smiles and runs off. I look into Jesus' beautiful blue eyes, and begin to cry. Touching his cheek I ask him to forgive me.

Looking down at my feet I notice I'm wearing sandals and a robe. He raises my head. "You are not Judas this time. You are a child like these around you. We have seen your service to these children. They have come to greet the children you will send back to my Father."

Jesus places a golden chain and medallion around my neck, and when I look down it dissolves into my chest. My chest feels solid, but now looks like golden liquid. I can smell toast and maple syrup, and I think of my nanna. This happens three times, and each time Jesus adjusts the chains, his hand melts into my chest while he says, "I baptize you the keeper of truth, I baptize you the bringer of faith, and I baptize you the protector of children."

When I look from my chest back to Jesus, he is no longer standing in front of me. He is on the other side of the valley, waving and smiling at me. Slowly, the valley dissolves, and I am back in my kitchen.

Not knowing what has happened, or why, I ask Gegu.

"Because you have been chosen," he replies.

Honestly, I don't know how to respond, or what I should feel. I think about the line from the movie, *Kindergarten Cop, "Is it a tumor?"* God, I hope not!

I feel disorientated and a little nauseous. With the smell of flowers still in my nose, I stifle a sneeze and wonder if I'm a little crazy. Jesus seemed too polished; too unlike the travel worn, tanned, poorly clothed and warm Jesus that first greeted me. And I wonder how *real* the experience was.

Gegu smiles and says, "Have faith."

ZEBEDEE

For some weeks I'd been thinking about Zebedee. Joachim and Miriam had both mentioned him, and I discussed Zebedee and Jesus' relationship with Gegu.

When I'm not working during meditation, I drift from image to image, and faces of spirits materialize like slides in a picture viewer. The faces and images are random, and I have learned this symphony is imprinting a recognition trigger onto my psyche—like a fingerprint or DNA left at the scene of a crime.

From this process I developed a sense of Zebedee. Gegu told me Zebedee had experienced prophetic visions similar to those attributed to Nostradamus. I was curious.

It is not easy trancing Zebedee. My body is too small for his giant frame—it's like *The Duke,* John Wayne, wearing Tom Cruise's flight suit in *Top Gun.* Zebedee has crazy, grey and silver hair, which flows into his full beard, and he's deceptively quick and athletic. He adjusts my posture and deepens my voice. I have a sense of the ocean while he uses my body. My eyes squint against the sun reflecting off the sea, and I am a little off balance trying to brace for the next wave.

Zebedee

"Well, young man, what can I say that will not hurt you? You have asked me to share what should not be shared. You have asked me to share what should not have happened, but alas, it did.

"A brother-in-law I took fishing, a fine young man, a handsome man, with eyes blue like the sea, his hair long and flowing, never tied back—a prince. All day long, he would smile and laugh.

"It was a day we should not have been on the sea. The clouds were already forming, and when I hesitated, Michael joked and laughed. He smiled and challenged me. "Come on, old man. I don't need your strength; I shall pull the nets in by myself." So challenged, I went.

"We were out only four hours when the storm rose up, more ferocious than any I had known. It was upon us in seconds. Our boat began to corkscrew and then, because we had no time to pull down the sail, it spun, and the mast snapped. Young Thomas, my deckhand, was lifted from the deck in a single motion, and just as I reached for the rudder, Michael was lost.

"Even above the fierce winds, I could hear the timber striking him. Never before had I heard a more sickening sound. I saw him go over the side, and launched myself after him. I had a hand on him almost immediately, and the other around a piece of the mast. Holding on tightly, I lifted him to me while I raged at the storm, "Let us live. Let the boy live. Please, God, let the boy live!" I hung on to him, my beautiful prince; my fist twisted in his robe, and pulled him tightly to me.

"For two days, I floated upon the water. Two nights fell, and two sunrises came, and all the time I talked to Michael, telling him how beautiful he was, how strong he was, telling him that he would have many children—and telling him that I would not let him go.

"Around me, the air was alive with lights and colors I'd never before seen: flying things with faces, and my family walking, beaten and bloodied, into raging fires. I saw crosses of gold, and upon each of them a young man—a young man who I later recognized as Jesus. The sky was as blood and the sea as fire, but I did not let Michael go.

"I saw things I could not comprehend. I saw my country on fire. I saw people clothed in I do not know what. I saw things flying that were not birds—I could not shut my eyes—and then I was lifted from the water.

"Still holding on to Michael, I was lifted skyward, but I could not see the face that was there. I could hear my country screaming, its people dying, their lives taken by things that reflected the sun, things that moved that did not need to be pulled by horse or donkey. I saw people holding sticks of fire—I saw my people dying.

"I was lifted heavenward, and Michael was standing there, and he held my hand—and then he was gone. My prince was gone.

"How can I explain the things I had seen? They were not from my world—they are from yours.

"A fisherman lifted my body from the sea, and I held on to Michael so tightly they had to cut his robe and his hair from my hand. His body slipped from their grasp, and sank beneath the waves.

"I lay in a fever for many days, and my Michael was gone."

I pause for a long time before I continued speaking as my body twitches with the force of Zebedee's pain.

"The boy Jesus was always clumsy on his feet, and getting tangled in my nets. Although he tried hard, he frustrated me, which is not my way—I have patience for the boys, and love and kindness.

"When Jesus grew older, I recognized him as the young man I had seen in my vision upon the sea, and I knew I had been shown a glimpse of the future he would bring.

"It was not he who heralded this future; those responsible were the people he had come to save. He did not merit death, and his family did not deserve to suffer.

"Although he took my sons, John and James, I resent him not at all—I love him. I have always loved him, as I have loved all my family.

"Do your work, young man, and I will watch over you while you write. Walk with God, my son."

Many years after this trance, I cried editing this passage; my composure undone by despair. In 2001, Zebedee stood beside me and his hand engulfed my shoulder. The light from the monitor highlighted the tear tracks on his cheeks, but he remained silent.

Gegu hugged Zebedee, and this gesture allowed him to let go of his pain. His hand glided from my shoulder, and when I turned to look at him, a miniature storm of golden clouds and vibrational flares faded. Mary joined us and hugged us all. She was dwarfed by Zebedee, but supported his sobbing frame effortlessly—David's sister taking pity on Goliath and helping him to his feet.

I'd seen what Zebedee saw on the sea while we were trancing. It is what I see every night when I turn on the television: tanks and jets, and soldiers and terrorists murdering innocent people.

As I shared his visions, it felt like an army of miniature snowmen travelled up my legs, and waves of grief engulfed me. Zebedee had earned my respect—he was indeed a giant.

Zebedee was a man who hung on to another out of love. The superhuman feat of hanging on to Michael, fighting rough seas and resisting hypothermia, caused Zebedee's mind to shift, and he saw the future.

What was unknown to Zebedee at the time was that Michael had died instantly when the mast struck him, and Zebedee himself had a near-eath experience. He was returned to the Earth with love, because that was how he had left.

THE CIRCLE AND MARY MAGDALENE

Narelle felt she had been guided to church the night we first met. When she looked into my eyes she knew I had been Judas. She already believed she had been Anna, Grandmother of Jesus, and had developed a friendship with Anita, who she believed (and I later confirmed) had been the disciple Peter.

Narelle also felt compelled to attend the meditation circle with Diane where she met a young couple, Sean and Stacey. With trance, I discovered Sean had been John's brother, James, and Stacey had been Mary Magdalene.

Through his association with me, Max was drawn into the group, and Joanne, who had been Ruth, completed this circle. Joanne met with members of the group socially, but never attended the formal evenings of meditation and trance. All of us had meditated with Diane, although some only briefly. I agreed with Narelle that a force had brought us together.

Is it coincidence we met, or is coincidence an event directed by God—a *John Woo* action scene, cleverly directed and edited so as to appear real? If you challenge me to state how it's possible that spirits who have lived in biblical times have been reincarnated to befriend me, here, *girt by sea*, my answer is simple—I don't know.

I believe that, collectively, everyone has lived every lifetime. The past-lives we recall in this lifetime have similar themes and resonate with what is happening in our lives now. I'm remembering Judas' lifetime, but anyone can remember those memories, and the information about Jesus' life.

Did we really live those lifetimes? By associating with me, everyone has clearer memories of past lives, and more profound meditations. I'm uncertain how this is possible.

Everyone in our group has worked with spirit: Narelle, Anita, Sean, and I are successful healers, while the others have occasionally used their healing gift. Stacey is a gifted clairvoyant, but because she is young, she lacks confidence.

What we all have in common is the ability to communicate with our guides. I had, over a period of weeks, tranced everyone's guides. While in trance I used phrases and greetings only known to each individual, and I was able to describe everyone's guide accurately—their physical appearance, clothing and mannerisms.

We started to meet each week for meditation. Tonight we are at Sean and Stacey's. Sean opens the circle with a prayer, and then Anita, who is leading the meditation, directs us to imagine we're surrounded by blue light.

Anita looks and dresses like a Romani gypsy; her hair is dark and untamed, and she smells like jasmine and hemp. He skin is flawless and the color of glazed scones, which softens her gangly greyhound-puppy physique.

She always says something mysterious, "When I woke this morning I hatched into the green dragon." Inexplicably, everyone believes it to be true. Possibly because the multifaceted shades of green and brown in her eyes exude sincerity and self-belief, or we're all characters in the movie, *12 Monkeys*.

In spiritual circles, colors are significant. There's a consensus amongst spiritualists that certain colors mean different things: healing, protection, peace, love, etc. I don't place much emphasis on colors because I have so many other stimuli to decipher. I agree, however, that the interpretation of color is part of the language of spirit.

After Anita's meditation I became aware that Moses had joined us. He wanted to speak to her. Anita had known for some time that she was connected to Moses in a past life, and I believed, with Gegu's help, that she had been Moses' wife.

During trance, Moses confirms this, and apologizes to Anita for leaving her and their three daughters. As I'm speaking I see Anita and the three girls being raped and mutilated by Egyptian soldiers. The scene is shocking and I experience Moses' pain. I feel nauseous, feverish, and my body shakes with tension and grief.

Anita relives the horror of that day, and is left shaken. Moses is distressed, and begs for forgiveness. He admits his actions were selfish, and wishes he had taken his family with him.

Anita feels that the experience of Moses apologizing to her has healed her, and I feel the burden of guilt lift from the spirit of Moses. Over time, wisdom has taught me that the burden of guilt has been removed, not only from Moses, but also from the collective consciousness of the earth. It's now the strangling hold of grief and shock subsides.

After the trance, everyone is able to contribute to the story of Moses and Anita. They have all seen a part of the story similar to how they see in meditation. The energy created by being together heightens our abilities and fine-tunes our connection with spirit.

Moses tells me that as a child and young man, God spoke to him. The dialogue, powerful and direct, caused him to have seizures. He was a half-breed, the son of a concubine, and was cast out of the royal family to live with slaves. He became a leader, escaped slavery, and waged guerrilla warfare on the Pharaoh's rule.

Over time he freed more slaves and pioneered a safe route through the desert and into Israel. He did not part the Red Sea, but masterminded raids against a powerful army, and operated a clandestine freedom passage across the Red Sea.

He is a motivational speaker, and asks his followers to exercise tolerance and compassion for all men—*love thy neighbor*. His eyes are lie detectors, burrowing into your soul. During my lessons with him, he analyses every thought and memory I'm engaging in my responses to him, and this is what he asks of his followers; absolute honesty, delivered with respect—*thou shall not lie*. I admire him. He is *The Terminator* of prophets, programmed to complete his mission, no matter what.

Mary Magdalene has replaced Moses at my side, and is waiting to speak. Her face is flushed and she keeps looking at her feet. Gegu places his hand on her back and holds her hand.

As I listen to the others speak, Mary Magdalene and Gegu talk to me, and what is being hinted at surprises me. Everyone stops talking when I turn on my note taker, and Mary Magdalene shares her story with us all.

Mary Magdalene

"Even as a child, I've always been attracted to Jesus. He had this way about him, and there were always children around him. They seemed to gravitate towards him, enchanted.

"I remember being nine years old. He was three, and I was looking into his eyes. There was something about them. He had this way of pulling your heart out of you and filling you with incredible peace.

"Miracles frequently happened around him, but mostly they were kept within the family. Each moment spent with Jesus while he was a child was special—it was his way."

Mary Magdalene hesitates, and I can feel her indecision. I swallow heavily, and my hands feel as if they are twisting the hem of a dress.

"I attended a party at Lazarus' home, where gatherings were common. When I wandered away from the noise, I stumbled into Jesus, who seemed to appear from nowhere. He was lightly tanned and dressed in a plain robe tied with hemp. His hands were calloused from working with stone, and he had grown a beard since I'd seen him last."

Here, Mary Magdalene pauses and giggles nervously. Jesus had startled her, and now steadied her with his dry, calloused hand. His touch took Mary's breath away.

"We walked away holding hands until we could hear no voices. It was a beautiful night, with lots of stars out.

"We kissed—I don't think I was very good ... you know ... with the teeth, and all. I was a twenty-three-year-old virgin, while he was seventeen, and I ... well, my girlfriends had told me about it ... but ... you know ... umm ... I hadn't even seen a man's ... umm ... We ended up on the ground. We were kissing, and I remember the rocks on my bottom ... it was ... quick. I don't think we were very good at it."

I can feel myself blushing. Love and sex are universal and timeless, and it didn't surprise me that I spoke in a *modern* way rather than what modern Christianity might expect of biblical times.

"He was gentle with me, and it didn't hurt, not really. I think it was his first time as well. After we ... well ... finished, Jesus put his head on my chest and cried. I didn't know anyone could be filled with so many tears.

"We fell asleep, and woke with the sun. Jesus was a gentleman, and walked me home, and this time, when we kissed, we managed to get it right. When I looked into his eyes, there was a touch of sadness there."

"I didn't see him again before he travelled. Eight months later, a month early, I gave birth to his baby boy. It was an easy birth. My waters broke, I lay down, and there he was. I named him Mark, and he became a fisherman.

"He was with me when they put Jesus on the cross, but I never told him who his father was. If the authorities had known, they'd have taken him from me.

"I never told anyone who the father was, but I think Lazarus knew ... yes, I think so, and also Anna—yes."

In Mary's culture, most girls married at thirteen. Mary's father, Lazarus, because he was a wealthy businessman and loved his daughter, hadn't forced her to marry.

Watching Jesus and Mary Magdalene together is like watching a pair of Emperor penguins. They are majestic and graceful, and their kind gestures pull at my heart. Their fingers glide towards each other, and when they touch, one of them closes their eyes and sighs, dipping their head delicately, as if in an ancient mating ritual. Watching, I feel like I'm holding my breath while falling into their shy eyes.

Lyrics from the song by Foreigner surface from my memory—*I want to know what love is, I want you to show me. I want to feel what love is, I know you can show me* ...The pop culture from my past has influenced how I mark milestones and moments in my life. Music and scenes from movies are emotive and have embedded themselves in my psyche.

Jesus had always loved Mary, but he was burdened by the knowledge that his life would be short. He did not wish to endanger a wife and child, and he had cried because he knew Mary Magdalene would bear his son, a son to whom he could never come home to.

Throughout his life he slept with many women, but he didn't have the insatiable appetite of his father. He had periods of celibacy when he travelled, and later when he was evading capture. He doesn't have an opinion about how Christianity has portrayed his sexuality or lack of.

He's a man and he enjoyed sex. Intimacy provided an escape from the tension that was a part of his life, turned off the flow of constant psychic information, and healed him. He's disappointed that the church, built on his legend, discriminates against homosexuality. He had friends who were gay—and he doesn't like that I'm using the word "gay".

"I had friends. All relationships formed by love and respect should be honored."

He chose not to marry because he was a gifted psychic, and although the timing of events weren't always known, he knew he'd die young, and endanger family and friends.

When I return home, Gegu and I kiss the children and pull up their blankets. Joanne is already asleep when I climb into bed. She is breathing deeply, and the light from the television dances across her bare back. Admiring the smooth skin on her thigh, I kiss her cheek and tell her I love her. She does not stir. I ask Gegu to hold my hand and put me to sleep, which he does. "Goodnight, Gegu."

As soon as I feel his hand in mine, my mind is still and my body twitches the tension away. Without his presence the energy from other spirits would agitate me and keep me awake.

"Goodnight, my son."

While I am driving home from work on November 3, 2000, Mary Magdalene asks to speak about her life again. She spent the day talking to Gegu while I worked.

Mary Magdalene has been waiting patiently all day, so when I arrive home, I settle myself downstairs with my note taker and let her use my body once again.

Mary Magdalene

"I married Lucha when my child was three years old; he was a good man, and a good father to Mark. He was a fine fisherman, with a fleet of three small fishing dhows, and he worked alongside Zebedee.

"When Jesus returned from one of his trips away, he came to see me. Our son was six years old, so Jesus would have been twenty-three. As he walked towards young Mark, he knew immediately that he was his son, and when he sat down, the boy climbed straight into his lap.

"At the time, I was heavy with child, my second to Lucha, for we already had young Rachael.

"When I looked up at Jesus and Mark, I did not see a man and a boy, only two boys, joyful in each other's company. Jesus had changed little; the skin on his face was still smooth, but there were a few lines around his eyes. He still had that magical way about him, and he still filled me with wonder.

"Jesus did perform many miracles, but not in the way they have been written. He is a powerful healer, and he has the gift of foresight. When Jesus fed the multitudes on the beaches of Galilee, he had advised the fishermen to go out early, and when they did, there were so many fish in the sea that you could have walked upon them. This had never been seen before.

"The fishermen fished frantically, but in their greed, they pulled in too many, and the smell of rotting fish hung over the town of Nazareth for days. This brought the desert vultures, and the gulls from the sea, and our days and nights were filled with the sound of their squawking and squabbling.

"Jesus felt guilt and shame for this terrible waste, and although it seemed that the Father's hand was responsible for this wonderful show of nature, I think that if Jesus had known of the outcome, he would not have shared it with the fishermen.

"I had three children to my wonderful Lucha: Rachael, David and Nathaniel. David later became one of the many disciples of Jesus who came after his death.

"Many people in Nazareth looked at me with loathing, as I had birthed a child out of wedlock. They were cruel to me because I would not reveal who the father was. That is a secret I carried to the grave.

"Mark became a fine fisherman, and by the time he was old enough to go to sea, Lucha had six small fishing boats.

"This was when my life was most beautiful: going down to the beach on clear summer days, when there was enough wind to fill the sails, and looking out onto the most glorious, blue patchwork quilt.

"Lucha and Zebedee often competed to see who could pull in the most fish, and when the winds were right, they'd race each other to the shore, laughing like young boys. This sight filled my heart, but not as much as the night with Jesus."

As I am typing this last line I'm overwhelmed by Mary Magdalene's sadness and I begin to cry. She stayed with me all night; her head rested against my shoulder as if I'm her big brother. Her brown hair smells like red gum resin, and I'm aching to kiss her. I feel confused.

She moves and wipes away my tears. Her hand feels warm, real, but when I reach for her hand my fingers grasp air. Heartbroken, my hand falls instead to the keyboard, like a butterfly with a broken wing.

On November 4, 2000, Joanne and I spend an enjoyable afternoon at Anita's. Over lunch, we talk about spirit. Anita gives me some healing to re-energize me because I'm fatigued from all the trancing I've done. Anita's hands are warm when she places them on me. Energy flows from them, tingling through my body, and I feel as if I'm floating. Smiling faces of spirit enter my consciousness and they tell me they love me.

Mary Magdalene is still with me, and I have grown fond of her. She is a gentle, elegant woman. Reclining in the passenger seat, I set up my note taker when Joanne and I leave Anita's. I trance as Joanne drives and remember nothing of the trip home until she stops for fuel. Mary Magdalene addresses Joanne by the name by which she knew her in her lifetime.

Mary Magdalene

"Hello, Ruth. We spent a lot of time playing together when we were children. Do you remember Grandmother Anna shooing us out of the kitchen so she could bake bread for the fishermen?

"We'd run barefoot to the beach together and dive into the water. With so many people always at Joachim and Anna's home, we rarely had to do chores, and were able to spend a lot of time together.

"When you were eight, I was eleven, and Jesus was a clumsy four-year-old. After he had been fed in the morning, we would take him for a walk down to the market. Here, we picked up fresh fruit and vegetables, trading with Grandmother Anna's bread.

"Joseph and Mother Mary often argued, and we'd escape to the beach with baby Jesus and watch the fishing boats as they came to shore.

"You were always shy, especially with the boys, and this is why we became such good friends. A lot of boys were interested in us, but we preferred each other's company. We had a lot of suitors, and although I think you had kissed before, I had never kissed until that night with Jesus. You are the only one I shared that night with. I never told you Mark was his child—we had not talked about the intimacy—but I think you may have guessed."

Mary Magdalene and I sigh, and there is a long pause before we speak, during which I can feel her fear building.

"Soldiers took us to witness Jesus' crucifixion, and then raped us beneath the cross, holding us down while they took turns."

Mary Magdalene hesitates, and Gegu shows me this shocking scene.

"It was a cruel, harsh time, and Jesus' deeds had sown fear and anger amongst his people. His miracles had been talked about and exaggerated, and people were afraid.

"The soldiers gathered many of his family and friends, for they wished to show everybody that Jesus was a liar and a false prophet, and had not come from God.

"You struggled fiercely, refusing to give in, while the soldiers raped you. Then, thankfully, you lost consciousness. It was different for me. I was terrified—too terrified to move—so I lay still, unable to protest, my courage frozen.

"The day was filled with rage and fear. As the last spear was thrust into the body of Jesus, Lazarus, our father, lifted us off the bloody ground. Mother Mary was in shock. She had been beaten, but not raped, and she covered your body with hers and sobbed uncontrollably.

"The disciples felt shame, unable to help their friend as the soldiers held them at bay. Many of them had been beaten, and Peter, who had been grazed by a spear, carried a bloody wound.

"Thankfully, my beautiful Lucha did not witness my disgrace, but the soldiers had taken your virginity from you, as well as your baby brother, and you did not recover for many years."

Mary Magdalene sighs, and rushes away from this memory before sharing another.

"My beautiful husband, Lucha, carried the burden of raising someone else's son. People in Nazareth turned away from him and scorned him because he stood by my son and me.

"He had an old fishing companion, Aramiss. On this day, Aramiss had a heart attack pulling up the nets. Mark was with Lucha, and he touched Aramiss on the chest, and seemingly brought him back to life.

"Lucha, a strong, powerful man, beat Mark mercilessly and ordered him not to show his gift again. The unrest surrounding Jesus had caused Lucha to be fearful for his son's life."

Mary had more to say, but I was pulled from the trance when the car stopped. I'm slumped in the seat, my limbs are heavy and I can't feel my hands. It takes me a while to work out where I am, and it feels like I've been in a dreamless sleep for hours. Joanne had also experienced the trauma of being raped, and with tear-filled eyes described what Ruth had suffered at the crucifixion.

Later, editing the transcript of the trance, I notice the description of the rape was not vivid enough to have caused Joanne's reaction. The energy created by trancing is a tangible force, and it is this energy that had caused Joanne to relive her own experience from Ruth's lifetime. Often, people in close proximity to me while I'm trancing experience the physical and emotional feelings I'm transmitting.

One month later, when I'm typing the transcript of Mary Magdalene's trance, I ask Gegu if she wishes to add anything. He replies, "She is here, my son."

"Hello Mary."

"Hello, Simon. For many years after my brother's death, I feared for Mark's life, and it was Lucha's love that protected us. He was a quiet, gentle man, yet so powerful, and he often stood up to the soldiers who defiled our village. Lucha never raised a hand, but I feel that if he had, he would have taken a life. He'd die for his children, and he would have died for Mark. He loved us that much.

"After what the soldiers had done, years passed before I could lie with him. He never lay with another, and when we did make love he was gentle, cradling me in his arms while I cried myself to sleep.

"I woke to find him looking out to sea with tears on his cheeks. He was always so strong for me, but now it was his turn to cry.

"It is a beautiful morning, Simon, a beautiful morning. Thank you for crying with me, and I'm sorry I always make you cry. God bless you, sweet man. God bless."

As she leaves, Mary Magdalene kisses my cheek, and her lips feel warm and moist. She walks away with Lucha and her family towards the beach, and they all turn and wave. Tears wash away Mary's kiss, and Gegu puts his hand on my shoulder.

Of all the spirits who have visited, Mary Magdalene always leaves me in tears. Why does she affect me so? I remembered why two days later.

I'd always assumed that no one would want to befriend Judas—friends with a traitor? How can such a man have friends or loved ones? Why had I not asked about the rest of Judas' life? Gegu was waiting for me to ask.

As Judas, Mary and Lucha were my best friends. When I visited Nazareth I'd meet Lucha on the beach. Mary Magdalene, the children, and I would help him unload his catch. They'd invite me to dine with them, and during these festive evenings I'd play with their children and imagine that my own childhood could have been this good.

Sadly, it wasn't, and when memories of my childhood ambushed me, Mary Magdalene kissed my cheek and made me blush, and Lucha joked with me to make me smile. During my frequent visits to Nazareth, Mary Magdalene and Lucha became my family. I loved them passionately, and to Judas' surprise, he was loved back.

Lucha, with divine intuition, and after Jesus' and my death, found my hanging body and cared enough to tend to my flesh. He and Mary grieved for my passing and were saddened to lose two people they loved.

"They held you in the highest respect. They loved you. You were Jesus' brother."

Jesus' brother? I feel like I'm drowning, not in water, but in two thousand years of blame.

When Mary Magdalene visits, it is not only her emotions I feel; it's mine. I become Judas, and with certainty I can say, "I love you, Mary."

LUCHA AND PETA'S GUIDES

This morning, November 5, 2000, it's still raining, and I'm unable to work, so Joanne and I drive over to Max's for coffee. Joanne chats with Max"'s wife, Peta, and Max and I go outside so he can smoke.

We chat about everything that has come through in the trances, and I greet Janu. He responds with, "Hello, little one." The responsibility I feel for this book weighs heavily on me, and I look to Max and Janu for confirmation and confidence.

"You burden yourself with doubt; faith is all you need."

Max and I talk about Peta, who thinks we're all crazy and calls this our "witchy-poo phase". She's a skeptic who scoffs at the notion of spirits. Gegu, Janu, and Jesus told us Peta had lived the lives of John the Baptist, Elijah, and Adam's Eve, but Max and I are neither foolish nor brave enough to mention this to Peta.

Peta is a great mum to two children, maintains a home, runs the office, screens Max's calls and should never be woken in the morning. You'd receive a better reception if you stepped on a brown snake.

She has to stand on tiptoes to kiss Max, she's still a competitive hockey player, has shoulder length brown hair, immense, expressive eyes and a kind heart. She's confident, speaks her mind and loves to party.

Max and I ask who Peta's guides are, and we both hear the answer at the same time: Mother Mary, Ruth, and Mary Magdalene. Max also knows that Peta has North American Indian, Yellow Feather, as a healing guide.

We're born into an energetic environment, and we inherit the dreams and fears of our parents, their strengths and weaknesses. The emotions, behaviors, and consequence of generations of family course through our energy fields. The moment our souls are earthbound our family and the generations before have already influenced our future.

The potential existed at my birth to become a trance medium, so I'd need a guide to teach me this skill. Everyone has guides: light beings, angels, and spirits; they're not always someone famous. It's more common that they've lived regular lives.

Often, the guide appears as a person with whom, from every life we have lived, we have had the strongest bond. It's easy for Gegu to open pathways of communication with me because we have been twins. He has also been my father, my mother, and a friend. My soul and Gegu's energy are vibrating at: *I remember you*, and *I love you*.

I know that in the time of Jesus, Peta had been John the Baptist, but I am unable to *see* a strong relationship between Mother Mary, Ruth, Mary Magdalene and John the Baptist. I know John had dined with Jesus and his family, but John's bond was stronger with the men than with the women in the family, so I ask Gegu to explain the connection between these women and Peta.

"Gegu?"

"Their connection is a Universal one. Peta has chosen to be a mother and a wife, and she is in place to be a source of energy for Max. Max can be a powerful healer if he wishes. It is the energy around him that will lead to the development of his gift.

"This energy is created by the love shared by Mother Mary, Ruth and Mary Magdalene. All their spirits have spent countless lifetimes together. The form Peta's guides have taken is what is needed not solely for Peta, but also for Max, and his connection with you.

"Together, the spirits of Max and Peta chose to be together in this life, and you too, my son, were included in this decision. Max is "the one who stands beside you", and Peta has been chosen to support Max. You had planned to meet in this lifetime for the work you must do.

"It is a shame that throughout Peta's life there have been events which have led her to dismiss what cannot be changed. You and Max chose this path with Jesus, and you have led the life best suited to connect emotionally to the time of Jesus. Max's friendship with you is not a coincidence; it is this friendship that allows him to stand with you."

"Thank you, Gegu."

I have introduced many people to their guides, but Peta is not interested. Peta's guides are happy to serve in silence. They may wish to speak to her, but they will wait patiently. Peta may not knowingly use her guides in her lifetime, but their support and presence will manifest as imagination, intuition, synchronicity, and opportunity.

Now, Lucha interrupts Max and asks politely if he can trance. He has been standing with Mary while Max and I have been chatting, and he looks relaxed and content. I wait until Joanne and I get home before I let him use my body.

Lucha

"Hello, Simon. I am pleased to be speaking to you. I have been waiting patiently. Thank you for helping my beautiful Mary.

"I was born in Jerusalem and raised in a merchant family whose wish was that I'd be content to join the family business, but I didn't care to be my father's bookkeeper. At seventeen years of age, knowing there were fishing fleets there, I set out for Nazareth, with all I needed slung over my shoulder, hoping for work.

"Arriving dirty and tired, and with only a few coins left from my father's purse, I found my way to the beach. There, repairing a small fishing dhow, was a wiry, bearded man with the funniest bowed legs I had ever seen. He looked me up and down when I asked for work, and, although at the time I could not fish, we ended up working together for many years.

"I had often seen Mary Magdalene walking on the beach with her child. Rumors of this harlot who slept with other women's husbands were common, but I took no note of them. She was beautiful. One day, after many shy glances whenever I passed her in the market, I invited her to sup with Aramiss and I in our cramped stone abode. We were both shy. I was surprised I had asked, and even more surprised when she agreed.

"After our evening together, Mary Magdalene often appeared on the beach to greet me when I returned from my early morning fishing. Every day our love grew stronger, until finally we were married.

"I loved young Mark like my own blood, and I never questioned Mary about his father, for I did not need to know. My respect and love for her was too strong, and as far as I was concerned, young Mark was my son now.

"Mary gave me three beautiful children, Rachael, David and baby Nathaniel. Mark, an enchanted child, was always bringing home small animals that needed care. He was quiet and gentle, and all creatures were drawn to him.

"One day, while fishing with Aramiss and myself, Mark showed me his powerful healing gift. Aramiss had fallen from chest pain while pulling in the nets, and I assumed he had died. Mark placed his hand upon his chest and brought him back to life. He was only twelve years old, and I was filled with wonder and dread as a golden glow surrounded Aramiss.

"In a terrible rage born of fear, I turned on Mark. This was the gift of Jesus, and I was so fearful for my son's life I beat him to the deck. Standing over Mark, I tried to choke this gift out of him. At my back, however, the golden glow touched me, and I loosened my grip. In my son's eye, there was sadness such as I had only seen before, in the eyes of Jesus.

"Two weeks later, I collapsed to the ground with a ruptured appendix. As I lay curled up in an agonized ball, Mark stood over me and begged to be allowed to heal me. There was so much anguish and love in his young face, and the tears ran like rivers down his smooth cheeks and onto my upturned face.

"'Please, Papa, please." I had never seen such an outpouring of love, and when he laid his hands on me, my pain was gone. Then he fell into my arms and we cried together. Clinging to each other, we rose and turned toward the sea where, seemingly on beams of sunshine, Jesus was walking towards us. I was fearful, but too shaken to move.

"I could still see the horizon through Jesus' body as he stepped towards us. He placed his hand on Mark's cheek and spoke quietly. "Do not be afraid, my son. The Father needs only one man for the cross. It is not your time." Then Jesus faded into the rising sun, and it was then that I knew Mark was Jesus' son.""

The images of Jesus walking on light seem unreal, and if I hadn't had similar experiences I'd have questioned the accuracy of this conversation. Seemingly out of nowhere, and during the weeks Jesus and his family visited, spirits and angels materialized around me. Friends, sometimes frightened, saw spirits standing beside me. As my faith grew, I no longer needed physical proof that spirits were real, and now I rarely see *solid* spirit. They are real.

"I respected Mary, and did not tell her that I knew that Jesus was Mark's father. Mark never used his healing gift again. He will always be my son, and I am thankful that his father released him.

"I was not present at Jesus' crucifixion. I was out on the sea, and when I returned home, I found my Mary disgraced and lying in Grandmother Anna's home. Anna had already passed away, but this was still her family's home.

"Mark was only sixteen, still a boy, and had witnessed the soldiers defiling his beautiful mother, and the helplessness he had felt weighed heavily on him.

"Mary cried for days, more for her son's pain than her own. Mark had known on that day he was watching his father die. He, too, had suffered terrible beatings, but he was young, and his wounds healed quickly. I loved my Mary for her courage. I helped her to heal, but it was twelve months before Mark was able to replace his hurt with the healing love he so desperately needed.

"We were all on the beach one morning, home from fishing, when we heard a shout and a splash as a young Arab girl jumped overboard from one of the larger trading dhows that frequented Nazareth. The Arab sailors had traded her for the smoking drug, and they had used her for their pleasure on the voyage.

"When she reached shore, she found herself in Mark's strong arms, and there she stayed. Her name was Nymphus. She gave Mary and me six beautiful, brown grandchildren; five girls and, the youngest, a boy. We named him Joseph, after Mary's cousin of Arimathea. He grew into a fine young man, and set out on a holy pilgrimage following in his grandfather's footsteps.

"Mary passed on three years before me. I buried her near the cove where we had first made love. There, sitting on our beach watching the sunrise, I met Jesus once more, and he and my Mary took me to heaven."

Ruth

On the evening of November 5, 2000, Joanne and I invite friends for dinner. While we are enjoying a lamb roast and drinks, Ruth, because she wishes to trance with me, distracts me. It's hard to pay attention to guests when another voice is in your head. I could ask her to be quiet, but I know she's excited. She has watched the other members of her family speak, and now it is her turn.

Ruth keeps apologizing for interrupting our dinner guests, but I'm the one responsible for her persistence because I won't ignore her. I'm able to communicate with her in my mind, but if I do, my guests will notice I'm ignoring them. Joanne knows what's happening; she catches my eye and smiles.

I'm aware of the sense of urgency as spirits, after having waited for so long to be heard, jostle for position. Gegu is the doorman, and Jesus, directing patrons to my table, is the maître d' of my restaurant; it looks like the evening has been over-booked.

Like slivers of rotating glass, spirits emerge from the painted walls of my living area, from the furniture, filling empty space, merging with décor and mouth-watering aromas. My imagination dresses for dinner and I create the atmosphere I desire:

Joseph is nursing a Bundy and talking to the beer-drinking John the Baptist, while the apostles are deciding whether to smoke with the Indian chiefs in the private booths. The Marys are dancing together, watched by Moses and his boys, the Red Sea Angels. Anything you need, they'll fix it for you—know what I mean. I think about the bar scene in *Star Wars*, and look for *Hans Solo* and *Chewbacca*.

Looking at Joanne, I wonder how, if Joanne's spirit had lived the life of Ruth, I'm able to communicate with and see Ruth? Working with the energy of spirit is like walking across a minefield of intelligent reasoning laid by an ardent, evangelistic-powered skeptic.

Gegu's answer is, "God is responsible." This may not satisfy the aforementioned skeptic, but, in my defense, I've never seen the ghost of Judas. Joanne has, though, and I'm pleased, because when people start to question my mental health she can join me at the asylum.

Ruth in spirit is like a hologram projected out of and into consciousness. A *veil* of fear prevents most people from being aware of spirit, which is sensible, because it would be difficult to live a human life if the world of spirit was always visible. What we see in our minds is also projected in the physical world, but it remains invisible. I can *think* Ruth into reality, but in this instance *God* is projecting Ruth—the real living

Ruth, not a Ruth altered by my consciousness—into my environment and mind.

Finally, Ruth's persistence is rewarded, and after our guests have gone and Joanne has put herself to bed, she gets her chance to use my body. Later, when I play the tape back, I'm surprised by her opening comments. Jesus is supporting and encouraging his family, but it's apparent Ruth has been listening to her family speak and is learning things about her family that she didn't know in life.

Ruth

"It surprised me to find out I was Jesus' half-sister. I never suspected it. Many things have surprised me, but it didn't change the love I felt for my family.

"My mother was fifteen years old when I was born, and ten months later, Rachael was born. My mother had no milk, and so Miriam nursed Rachael.

"It was too soon for my mother to fall pregnant again, and in her depressed state, she was unable to cope with two young babies. I never realized it then, but now, after what I have heard, I believe my mother was feeling guilty because of what had happened between her and Lazarus.

"I'm confused about Miriam, always so strong and composed—or so it had seemed. Joseph's behavior was inexcusable, but it's difficult to lay blame, for I respected my family, and loved each member dearly.

"I remember my mother returning with baby Jesus. I got under everyone's feet because I wished to hold the baby. I wanted to hold my new brother, and when, eventually, I was given my chance, he felt so warm and lovely in my arms.

"I was only a toddler myself, and not strong enough to hold him, so Grandmother Anna made me sit on the ground with him. It was then that I heard his singing voices.

"Jesus and I spent a lot of time with each other when we were growing up. Mary Magdalene was my best friend, and so we were often together. We dragged baby Jesus with us everywhere. We were happier together, and exciting things were always happening.

"Mary Magdalene's father was Lazarus. His home was outside the township of Nazareth, a forty-five-minute walk from home. Lazarus had a large plot of land with stables for his horses and a yard for camels and donkeys, and his home was twice the size of Joachim and Anna's, with a large covered area where he stored his goods for trade.

"I remember soothing baby Jesus when he was seven. He'd often have trouble sleeping, and he always used to say that someone was talking to him. I never believed him, but on this night a beam of light came through the window and illuminated us. He wasn't scared, but I was terrified. He put his hand in mine and said, "It's all right sister. It is only my angel." I cannot describe the form in the light, but knew only there was something there.

"As time went on, these events became common—each member of the family experienced at least one. Jesus radiated light, but it was more than a glow of happiness—he was different, and I loved him.

"When I was sixteen and suffering badly with menstrual pain, Jesus was twelve. Talking about it makes me blush, but on this occasion, Jesus looked into my eyes while holding my hand, and suddenly my cramps were gone.

"One day, while we were walking away from the settlement, we stumbled across an old street hag who had been made homeless, and the most amazing thing happened. I never knew where these old crones came from, or where they had been, but they always seemed to have their hands out waiting to be fed.

"I didn't want to go near her, but Jesus walked up to her and looked into her eyes. He told her there was no need for her to smell this bad and lie around in the shade like a mangy dog. He touched her lightly on the forehead and whispered some words I couldn't catch.

"She had one milky eye and visible septic sores. I couldn't bear to be near her for the smell of her rotting flesh, but then I noticed a scent—the sweet fragrance of the desert flowers that grew after the infrequent rains of spring and summer. I looked around to see a golden mist, and heard voices singing, but not words that I knew.

"When I glanced down at the old lady again, her face looked younger and her sores were gone. She still wore the same smelly rags, but her crippled fingers had been straightened, the sores on her face had healed, and her eye was clear.

"She had beautiful green eyes of an uncommon color. As I stared, I realized how beautiful she was—I was seeing her the way Jesus did. This was how he saw everybody. This was his gift.

"I'd often find him sitting alone sobbing. I would hold his hand and ask what the matter was. He'd have no answer, so I'd kiss his baby cheeks and hold him tight. I loved him dearly.

"Jesus started working with Joseph when he was eleven years old. I don't think he enjoyed it, but he tried his hardest. The funny thing was, James and Jude were younger than Jesus, but they were already working."

"Jesus was too busy with Grandmother Anna and Mother Mary. He was a shy child, and Mother Mary, knowing he was special, had tried to keep him away from the influences of Joseph, for she knew Joseph's heart was tainted. Even I was aware of his cheating when I was growing up, but there came a time when she could no longer protect Jesus, and he went to work with his father.

"Jesus' brothers were always teasing him. Even when he was in his teens, they could still bring him to tears. At other times he was confident, and although I never saw him lose his temper, he could be forceful. Jesus had many shifting moods—he could be ecstatically happy, then uncomfortably shy. No matter what his mood, however, he was my brother, and I loved him.

"I thought I knew what had happened between him and my friend Mary Magdalene. She said they had only kissed, but when young Mark was eight or nine, I recognized Jesus in his eyes.

"In the years Jesus was away, I missed him terribly. One time, he was away for three years, which was hard for me. I was shy, and resisted the men who were interested in me. With Jesus, I felt alive, and it is fair to say that, as young adults, we shared a sexual attraction. He was the only man who could stir me, and there had always been warmth and comfort between us.

"I met all the disciples. My favorites were Peter, John, and James, and I think these were also Jesus' favorites, although maybe that is unfair of me, because Jesus loved everyone.

"A week before his crucifixion, there was a lot of unrest in Nazareth. Soldiers invaded homes, turning up tables and throwing possessions onto the street. Many people were beaten, and there was a lot of fear. The people of Nazareth gossiped and turned against him.

"Soldiers took our family to see the death of my beloved baby brother. Mother Mary, James, Jude, Lazarus and Mary Magdalene, Miriam, Rachael, and I were taken from Nazareth, and we didn't know where Jesus was.

"While being led to the site of the crucifixion, we were kicked, shoved and thrown to the ground. The only disciple I remember seeing there was Peter, because he was wounded, but I don't remember much after we had been taken from our home.

"When I finally saw Jesus, he had been whipped and beaten. One soldier was urinating while another held Jesus' head so the stream would splash into his eyes. I ran forward to help my brother and was caught and thrown to the ground. I fought as hard as I could, but soldiers pulled my arms behind me and ripped my clothing from my body. I kicked and screamed, rolled and twisted, but they held my legs and forced themselves into me. All I could smell was their stinking bodies as they grunted like pigs above me. The fourth or fifth pushed his forearm onto my throat until, fighting to breathe, I slipped into unconsciousness.

"I don't remember much after that until finally, when I was able to think clearly again, I was home. I remember crying for days and days … just crying."

When I listen to the last passages on the tape, *I* too am swallowing heavily, and begin to cry. On the tape, Ruth had said she lost consciousness after the second soldier raped her, but while I am typing she prompts me to write that it was after the fourth or fifth.

The hardest thing for me is that while in trance I'm able to feel the assault, both physically and emotionally. Now I feel like showering and scrubbing myself under scalding hot water, for it feels like insects are crawling across my thighs and buttocks. Is it body lice from the filthy soldiers, or spent semen? Ruth is beside me, and I hear her say, "I'm sorry."

Admiring Ruth's courage, I'm humbled and sorry for her pain. Ruth, nudging me when I made a mistake, stood bravely beside me when I typed her trance. She kept me warm, and her pride has prevented her from crying.

I don't know what I typed or thought, but now Ruth is crying, and the tears fall from both of us. We are both overwhelmed with grief. Gegu comforts us. His solid chest a pillow for my soul, and his love pulses in time with the ringing bell calling his brother monks to pray.

The energy and violence being shared with me is taking its toll. I'm disturbed by what I'm seeing and feeling, but these are the stories Jesus wants shared.

I've woken this morning, November 6, 2000, feeling drained. My feet are sluggish, and something is wrong with my eyes. They are sensitive to light and ache constantly. This is made worse by my burrowing fists trying to kill the hedgehogs wrestling on my irises.

Gegu tells me it has something to do with the spiritual energies I'm using in trance. My physical body is not conditioned to the environment created around me when I am trancing—I'm a footy player without match fitness trying to play a grand-final.

Despite all this, I cannot describe to you the force that drives me: I cannot say no to Jesus and his family. The weight of responsibility I feel towards Jesus and Gegu pushes me forward—the stories from the members of Jesus' family energize and motivate me to continue.

The weight of Judas' betrayal shackles me to this feeling of responsibility, and I wonder if it is because I feel I deserve to be punished that I have to endure the painful memories of Jesus' family.

Ruth is here again. She looks deeply into my eyes when I clip the note taker to my t-shirt. Our eyes become locked together in an epic battle; queen takes knight, and understanding pulls me into her glowing pupils. This time, we are in the car, and Ruth speaks while Joanne drives to school to pick up Scott and Lee. Joanne's arm reaches for the radio as my eyes close. *Kryptonite* by 3 Doors Down is playing. *"I took a walk around the world to ease my troubled mind. I left my body laying somewhere in the sands of time ... "* and that is my last memory before returning to Nazareth.

Ruth

"Once, going to the markets with Jesus and Mary Magdalene, Jesus became distressed. He was six years old. I found him standing, shaking and quietly crying. Tears were running down his cheeks and he had wet himself.

"I looked around to see what had disturbed him so, but I couldn't see anything. Crouching in front of him, I pulled his face to mine and started to cry with him. I swept him into my arms, but he fought against being embraced and stared over my shoulder, mesmerized. Feeling something behind me, I quickly spun around. All I saw were people going about their business; nothing seemed out of the ordinary. I couldn't identify what had made me so edgy, and I didn't know what Jesus had seen.

"Standing with his little body shaking in my arms and his wet robe against me, I tried to comfort him as best I could, but his tears continued to wet my shoulder. Turning again, I saw Mary Magdalene running towards us. She always knew when something was happening to Jesus and me. She had a panic-stricken look on her face and asked me if I had seen it? I was perplexed. I didn't know what she was talking about. She asked if I had seen the big black vulture that had cast a shadow over the market. I hadn't. Jesus had seen something, but I didn't know what it was.

"Together, we carried Jesus down to the beach where I stripped off his robes and cleaned him in the sea. It took him a while, but he eventually recovered. I washed his robe, and lay it over some rocks to dry. We walked along the beach while Jesus played in the water, having changed from being terrified and crying into the happy boy we knew so well.

"On another occasion when Mary Magdalene visited, when Jesus was seven, or maybe closer to eight, we ran to the beach together after my chores for Grandmother Anna were done. There was a cove where we could take off our clothes without being disturbed and go swimming. Jesus was a good swimmer, and he continued to swim after Mary Magdalene and I had dried and dressed.

"Then I heard the funniest sound. It took me a while to realize it was the squeals of dolphins. Jesus was still swimming, and all around him was a pod of fresh-water dolphins. I looked to my friend Mary, who was smiling with delight. We took our clothes off again and ran back into the water. Jesus was all giggles, ecstatic, and the water appeared to glow where we were swimming.

"I have many stories like this to share. We took them for granted, and it is only now, when talking to you, that I see how exciting they are. I will be back."

Ruth exits my body and leaves me warm and smiling. I thank Ruth and watch her long hair swaying in time with her womanly hips as she walks away. I'd wolf whistle if I knew how, or was younger and still wore my shepherd's whistle around my neck.

Ruth has been watching me type, and I have made her smile and blush. She punches me playfully in the shoulder when I lean back from the computer. My old farm dog, Tip, now in spirit, flops onto my feet when I think about the shepherd's whistle. Ruth's hot breath on my neck makes me think about turning and kissing her on the cheek.

On December 19, 2000, I'm proofreading what I've written when Ruth arrives again. She wishes to talk about her life after the crucifixion, but I am too tired. "I'm sorry, Ruth. If you return tomorrow I will be fresher."

"That's okay Simon. Congratulations. It will be a boy." Ruth kisses me, and smiles goodbye. Joanne is five weeks pregnant, and we are hoping for a boy.

Well, tomorrow has come, and Ruth has been with me all day, listening to Max and I talk. I have enjoyed her company, and look forward to trancing with her again.

Ruth

"What horrors I endured at my brother's death. What was most sacred was taken from me, but later I found love and happiness, and eventually I would marry.

"Forty days after my brother's death, he visited me. He came while I sat at the table we had so often shared, talking to our grandmother and enjoying her baking, listening to our mother's sweet voice and watching her smile.

"I was sitting by myself in the lamplight crying. Suddenly he was seated opposite me. His hands felt warm, and they were alive; was he alive?

"When I went to speak, he placed his hand on my lips and said, "Hush, my sister. What beauty I see before me, and what sadness and pain you are carrying. I have come to take that from you. You will not endure that day, and you will not be visited at night by the demons that haunt you. I have taken them away, sweet sister.

"'For so long, you have watched over me. For so long, you have held me in your arms. Even until recently, before my death, did I cry on your shoulder. Not once did a harsh word pass between us, and now it is my turn to watch over you.

"'I am strong—stronger than I have ever been—I am more complete, and I shall bring a man to you; a man for you to marry. Though you shall not have children, you shall be surrounded by light, and whenever you wish, you only have to ask, and I shall be there.'

"He took his hand from my lips and held my face and wiped my tears. He sat with me for many hours, and we talked and laughed about our childhood. Good memories. Good memories.

"My brother guided me to you. My brother stands beside you, and he is thankful for all that you do. Thank you again for sitting alone and comforting me. God bless you, Simon."

JESUS

Today, November 6, 2000, I am with my friend, Helen. While we are talking, chills run across my shoulders. Smiling, I ask Gegu who wishes to speak to me. "It is her guides," he replies. In this situation I ask Gegu a series of questions, which helps me to connect and communicate with new spirits.

"How many guides does she have?"

"Three, my son."

"Are they all men?"

"No, my son. Two men, and one woman child." Gegu often uses child as a term of endearment. I'm Joanne's "man child," and she's, "gentle one."

"Who is her main guide?"

To my surprise, I am introduced to Pontius Pilate. After the formality of the introductions, Pontius Pilot tells me he wished to spare Jesus from the cross, but his and his family's lives were at risk. He never spoke to Jesus when he was captured. Cowardice and fear kept him away. Minions were ordered to torture and crucify Jesus, and Pontius Pilot, fearful of the angry mob, remained in his quarters.

I ask Jesus why his conversations with Pontius Pilot in the Bible are recorded differently. He smiles and shrugs his shoulders, "It's not important, brother." When questions about the authenticity of the stories in the Bible enter my mind, Gegu and Jesus smile and direct me to not wonder. Jesus' family, life, and connection to his Father are important to him, not the Bible or the evolution of Christianity.

Helen had been a member of the Sanhedrin who had argued in defense of Jesus, which made her part of the minority. Not many of the Sanhedrin had supported Jesus, and in the end it was his own people who condemned him.

The list of people I know who are a part of this story continues to grow. Helen works for a law firm, and I have met a secretary there who was Judas' mother. The moment our eyes met I recognized her. She had Judas' mother's eyes. Her body shape and physique are the same, and even her hair is identical in terms of color and style.

It was an awkward moment, and for a second we both hesitated. I recognized her immediately, but she didn't understand what was happening and looked flustered. Every time I went there afterwards, even though I was there for professional reasons, I felt she wanted to linger and talk. It reminded me of the goofy teenage stage of wanting to talk to a girl, but you weren't brave enough.

It was difficult, though. What could I say: "Hi, two thousand years ago I was Judas and you were my mother. Oh, and by the way, you were a prostitute and a drunk. Hang on, there's one more thing: your husband, my father, used to beat the crap out of us. But it's okay; I'm going through a forgiving period in my life. Would you like to have coffee with me?" I think some things are best left unsaid.

It is surreal, though, being around her. She is a lovely person, and I wonder if the electricity between us is caused by what is happening to me spiritually. I don't think of her as being Judas' mother, but it's strange knowing she had been.

After my meeting with Helen, Jesus arrives and keeps me company during the morning. He seems thoughtful, and it appears he is looking for something, or someone. He comes home with me and waits patiently while I have lunch with Joanne.

Jesus

"Hello, Simon. I have come because my sister Ruth has been speaking to you. She told you of the time in the market place when I was six years of age. I was often with Ruth and Mary Magdalene, and holding a hand each, they'd swing me between them on our frequent outings.

"We had gone to the market on an errand for Grandmother Anna. There were many people in the market that day. The mood was happy and joyous, and I pulled free from Ruth's hand. She paid me no mind because everyone in the community knew us, and she knew I would be safe. We were the grandchildren of Anna, the one who baked the most delicious bread.

"As Ruth went about her chores for Grandmother, I wandered around and looked at the stalls, speaking to a donkey and a street dog that ran to greet me. I always liked animals, and they enjoyed my attention.

"Suddenly, my stomach became unsettled and it felt like I was being smothered, like when you get tangled in your blankets and you can't get out. I turned and saw a man looking at me. He was staring at me rather keenly, and I felt I knew him somehow. My legs were heavy as I started to walk towards him, and although he was making me nervous, I was drawn to him.

"Two forces seemed to be controlling me—the scrutiny of the man pulled me towards him, while another force was trying to hold me back. When I got close enough to see into his eyes, my feet refused to move any further, and planted themselves firmly on the ground. The man crouched down and started to change; his eyes turned red, his teeth became fangs, and my legs were frozen with fear.

"Looking around, it was obvious that no one else could see him, for everyone in the marketplace was acting normally. When I looked back the man was still there, and then it was as though he was coming towards me without actually moving; this power rushed towards me, through me, then up and away, and he was gone.

"My mind was clear, yet my body betrayed me, and I felt the wet warmth of my fear dripping down my legs, and tears streamed from my eyes. The next thing I remembered was Ruth holding me in her arms. I knew she was crying, so I reached out to her, not with my hands, but with something else; something I didn't understand.

"Ruth took me to the water and washed me, and she has told you how we spent the rest of the day together. It ended up being a beautiful day.

"There is a force that opposes the love of my Father and His will—a force created by the evil deeds of men. My Father, in His wisdom, offered you free will, and you have always chosen the easy path, the path of hate, fear and disbelief. The harder way is the path of love and forgiveness, but the rewards are great.

"Always, there is balance in life, but the un-balancer of this world is man, and you do this with your free will and your lack of faith. The mind is powerful, and it can overcome many things. It can overcome love, and it can overcome faith. You have forsaken your connection with my Father.

"All men who have this connection with my Father are watched equally by the Father and the other, and so what I experienced at the market was the full force of the watching eyes that would wish upon me not death, but the unleashing of evil that is more often than not the path of free will.

"Ruth has described the night she first saw my angel. I'm not sure when I first realized that someone was there. Up to the age of four or five, I thought it was my mother or Grandmother Anna who had come to soothe me. Unable to stop the voices in my head, I used to have frequent nights of restless sleep and tears.

"By the time I was five, I realized my visitor wasn't anyone who lived in our home. She glided gracefully, materializing from the light, draped in glowing white cloth. When she held her arms up, it looked like she had wings. As I grew into an adult, I believed I was seeing wings; not feathered wings but energy and light, a blanketing of love that, at times, formed the shape of a giant wing.

"Her name was Ellueshion, a name that teased your senses and sounded like wind heard from a distance. She comforted me when I was disturbed.

She quieted the voices in my head, taught me how to understand them, and how to be brave. One of the voices was my Father's. I know you hear it as a language, or perhaps I should say *feel*, as we both have an understanding of this, but I, as a child, did not.

"She made me feel joyous. My mind was clearer, and my fear was held at bay. This feeling was the peace that Eastern cultures strive to achieve with meditation. But remember, at the time I was only a child, and I was happy simply to be able to go back to sleep.

"I knew Joseph's heart. He was a deeply religious man, but his religion was the gospel of his voice, not the feeling of his heart. He preached many good words, and outwardly he showed people good conduct, but he was always overcome by the temptations of lust.

"I did not resent him; I loved him. He was my father, and I understood his way. The sadness for him was that it was a constant battle between faith and guilt, and his soul has lived many lives trying to balance these.

"I sensed his deceit with Miriam. It cost her dearly, this indiscretion with Joseph, but she had been drawn into his web, seduced by the passion and the risk. She had a fine relationship with her husband Zebedee, but she missed the excitement of their youth.

"She forgot the things that were important to her: the effect of Zebedee's deep throaty voice, his gruff laugh and his weathered strength. She took things for granted, as many of you do today, and when she was overcome by her actions, she never again trod the path of infidelity. She could never release her guilt, though, because her sons reminded her of Joseph.

"James and John had good hearts. We were the best of friends. I, too, believed they had a strong connection with the Father, and when I returned from my travels, they came with me to walk this path. It was a path of enlightenment, of faith and truth, but it was also a path of pain.

"I had a strong bond with my Mother. The love she felt for her children was admirable. I know she had powerful spiritual experiences, but they caused her a great deal of fear. Her gift was foreseeing what lay ahead—both joyous and painful.

"Her sanctuary was the memory of the night with Lazarus. This was her way of crying out for help, for Joseph caused her heartache. She always loved him dearly, but he was so full of guilt that he was harsh with her.

"In a way, I was my mother's protector. Joseph was gentler when I was with them, and when our eyes met, I could see his fear. He knew I had an understanding of him, so I could caution him, caution his heart, and my mother drew strength from this.

"She was always busy; there were many mouths to feed. She not only mothered her own family, but was also a mother to Miriam's family. She carried a lot of guilt from being unable to feed young Rachael, who was raised in Miriam's household after sharing the breast with James. Rachael and James formed a keen bond from this shared feeding.

"The deceit (Miriam's affair with Joseph) between Mother Mary and Miriam drew them closer. It is strange how these things work; that a lie would serve to reveal the love they shared.

"When I was nine years old my brother James, who was six, and Jude, who was five, were away for the day with Zebedee. This was his way, to take all the boys out when they were this age. I was not comfortable on the sea, and my clumsiness had been my downfall with Zebedee.

"Zebedee was an active fisherman during this period, but there came a time when he was not, and the family moved to Capernaum. He was frugal with his money, but because he was generous with his heart, wealth would eventually come to him.

"On this day, Mother Mary, Miriam, my sisters Ruth and Rachael, and baby Hannah set off to Lazarus' home. Lazarus had many homes, and this one was outside the township. This was where he resided when he needed some peace and quiet.

"Lazarus was an influential figure within the Magdalene's. He was a trader and a merchant. Goods passed through his hands and across his desk. He had many people working for him, and was also uncommonly generous.

"When his wife passed, he was left lonely, grief-stricken, and unable to smile. It was during this time that he often chose to leave his home in Bethany and come to Nazareth.

"This journey took him two days. There was no need to drive the horses, mules or camels hard, for depending on how early he left in the morning, he'd always arrive before the second night.

"Preparing to travel, we hitched our faithful old donkey to the cart and set off to see Lazarus. Unbeknownst to our father, we had named our donkey Joseph, because he was a stubborn, obnoxious, smelly beast.

"It took us only half an hour to reach his house this day. On the way, I lay in Rachael's arms and looked up at her face. She had a funny little dimple, a bit off center on the point of her chin. Smiling and winking, she looked down at me with her beautiful brown eyes. Her hair was always an unruly mess, curly, free, and wild. I cherished these moments the most. Mother Mary's joy was infectious, and distracted us from the heat of the day.

"When we arrived at Lazarus' house, he was watching his yard boys tidying the yard and sweeping out the stables. His horse, a short stocky desert stallion, was lame. It was an impressive horse, and Lazarus loved it a lot, but now its right front leg was held off the ground. Lazarus, concerned for his horse, was bullying the yard boys. They paid him no heed. Smiling, they continued on with their work, their cheeky brown faces unconcerned.

"Lazarus enveloped Mother Mary and Miriam in his arms, and they kissed him affectionately before pushing him towards the stables. I ran past them and slipped under the rope across the stable door. The stallion shied away, but I looked up at him and smiled. As was the way with animals and myself, we talked—in horse language, of course—and then suddenly I was in tears, overcome by a feeling flowing through me.

"I knew the horse felt love for his master. Lazarus quietly approached, lamenting over what to do, as he had found no stone in his stallion's hoof. I could feel the outpouring of Lazarus' love. I breathed in then blew into the horse's nostrils. Quivering, he threw his head up so quickly that I was thrown backwards, landing in an untidy heap on the ground.

"I was now crying tears of joy, and laughing hysterically. Lazarus was the first to reach me. He was a strong man, and after he plucked me from the earth and brushed me down, he looked into my laughing face and couldn't help smiling. Now, he was able to release his grief for Ruth. He cried and cried, and held me tightly, holding me so close that I could smell his man scent and feel his strength. This is what Joseph had never done for me.

"Miriam wept, and Mary hugged us all. Rachael stood with her hands on her hips, smiling unconcernedly. She was a funny little thing, and could not see what the fuss was all about. When we had all calmed down, I held Lazarus' hand and led him to his horse. "It is all right, he is fine." And sure enough, he was standing proud. Everyone was quiet. There was love all around us, and everyone was crying.

"I was always a soft child, more at ease with Grandmother Anna and Mother Mary than with the men. I'd help Grandmother Anna with her baking, and Mother Mary with the spinning of fibers and sewing. I was happiest doing chores in their company, or spending time with Rachael, Ruth, and Mary Magdalene.

"When Rachael was free from her duties, we talked and played together whenever we could. One day we found a small cave, and we took bread, blankets and anything else we could find to play at being grownups. Sometimes, we lay naked together, pretending in the way of children, and I'd marvel at her softness, and enjoy her spirit.

"It was different around my brothers. James and Jude liked to tease me, and even though I was older, they often brought me to tears with their harsh words.

"As is the way of boys and siblings, we had many battles, wrestling each other to the ground. It's not that I always lost, but whenever I was able to be aggressive enough to hold them in the dirt, it left me drained, and when they cried the dust out of their eyes and looked down at their broken fingernails, torn robes, and scuffed knees, it was too much for me to bear. The way of boys growing up is to yell, push and shove, throw rocks and dust, run … but it was all too much for me. It was torment. My heart was too soft to keep up with my brothers.

"My brothers had already travelled and worked with Joseph for three or four days at a time while Joseph read scripture, did some carpentry, or worked with stone. James had first gone when he was seven, and Jude followed when he was six.

"Mother Mary and Joseph argued about why my mother was keeping me home. She kept me close to her, for she knew of my softness, and of my gift. I believe that all the women in our family were blessed with my Father's sight.

"The moments I spent with Ruth and Mary Magdalene, and those with Rachael, when we pretended to be husband and wife, became most precious to me. They distracted me from the voices in my head, and from the flow of emotions that frequently overpowered me and caused bouts of crying.

"It was hard for me to be alone amongst the people of Nazareth. From the age of seven or eight, when I first knew of such things, I always knew who was cheating or stealing. But worse than that, I felt the hatred and the anger. I'd become agitated, and not know what to do, end up crying. When I was with the girls, however, their love and joy saved me from this heartache.

"When I was eight years old, my father Joseph beat me because I had taken his smoking tobacco. I had taken it for my games in the cave with Rachael, and when he asked, I lied. James knew I had taken it, and even though we fought, and he teased me, he did not betray me. James was always in trouble; knocking things over and slow to move whenever Joseph was around, and when Joseph turned on him, I confessed.

"Joseph had been away for three or four weeks. When he returned he was tired and dirty, bad tempered and guilt ridden. Mother Mary had turned away from him because of the stink of the women on his flesh. He argued with Grandmother Anna. He took all this out on me, tearing my robes and giving me a beating. Because he was in a tremendous rage, when I twisted and broke free, he picked up a wooden ladle and struck me on the arms and legs. Once again, I wet myself from fear. As I lay waiting for the next blow, Joseph was suddenly lifted from me. I looked up to see Zebedee holding Joseph in his giant paw, his hard eyes stilling any protest. For some reason, he had come home, and as he held Joseph, he said not a word.

"Grandmother Anna tended to me and lifted me to my feet before leading me to the stable where she bathed me. Her lovely, sad face was wet with tears, and her gentle hands were shaking. I lay against her, wet and naked. Together we cried.

"Sometime later, my mother found us sitting in the shade. She had been crying; her eyes were red and swollen. We sat together quietly, and were gradually blanketed in a golden glow. No words passed between us, for no words were needed; we loved each other. I know that, at those times, Grandmother Anna missed her Joachim. He was always the happy, smiling one, sitting us all down for dinner and making us laugh.

"Later that evening, I woke to the sound of my parents coupling, and I wondered at the strength of my mother's love for her family and her marriage, for she never turned away from her Joseph. Her love was always forgiving and complete, and only my Father, your God, was her equal."

When I type the record of this trance, I feel like a voyeur, as if I have looked into a window of a home when I had no right to do so. Jesus fades away, and I thank him for this honor and leave him to his memories. I know he will be back, and I am humbled by this thought. Exhausted, I lean back into Gegu, who hugs me. I begin to cry.

"It's all-right, my son. He loves you. We all do."

The next morning is November 7, 2000, and I wake up feeling hung over. I keep looking over my shoulder because I can feel someone or something watching me. It's not Jesus or his family because he is looking, too. Gegu is relaxed, and Moses, who has been talking to me today, smiles reassuringly.

I trance with Jesus again, but I have trouble disengaging from my body, and I hear the first sentences before I sit with Gegu.

Jesus

"It is all right, Simon. Take your time. I will allow you to sleep tonight. You will sleep with angels. Let's clear your mind so we can trance.

"I was nine years old. My father Joseph was preparing to travel. On this day, we were bound for Capernaum. My mother joined us, along with Ruth, Rachael, and James, but not Jude; he had stayed behind with Miriam. Hannah, Rachael and Grandmother Beth were also accompanying us, for Grandmother Beth had family in Capernaum.

"The journey was pleasant enough, for the day was fine, and I was enjoying the company of my sisters and our cousin. Mother Mary and Joseph were talking to each other, happy and smiling. When he was doing God's work, he was always like this.

"There was a gathering place close to the shore, a small place of worship where wise men met; community leaders, elders, academics, and men of faith. When we arrived, Joseph joined the gathered men and participated in their debate. They argued rules of law and land title, contested scripture, and vied for position amongst themselves.

"I stayed with my mother and sisters close to the shore. Grandmother Beth, accompanied by Ruth, had gone in search of her family. It was then that a force seized me and threw me to the ground. I didn't know what it meant. It was as if a giant hand had pushed me to the earth. I looked skywards, and could see a light coming towards me. I was afraid, and my legs and arms were twitching as though I was having a fit.

"Mother Mary grabbed my hand, and Hannah started to cry. Rachael yelled, "What should I do? What should I do?" and ran to get Joseph. I could see light flowing straight into me, but I didn't think anyone else could see it.

"Joseph and some of the other men came rushing over, alerted by the commotion. With them was a strange looking man, tall and thin, with long fingers, beady eyes and a funny, squeaky voice.

"He looked down at me and placed his hand on my chest. Pushing my mother aside, he pulled me roughly to my feet. "Behold, the Messiah has come. Behold, it is the Son of God." I was more frightened of him than I had been of the light. He hugged me tightly and spun around in circles, then lifted me up high above himself. "You are the one. You are the Messiah. You are the Messiah of whom John the Baptist spreads the word. You are the Messiah rising from the scriptures of Moses. Behold!"

"He continued to hold onto me, and dropping to his knees, he said, "Quickly, we must pray." The other men looked bemused, while my mother stood still, eyes wide and mouth agape. Rachael settled Hannah. James, who had been further down the beach, ran back to us looking bewildered.

"Eventually, Joseph persuaded this man, Simeon, to release me, and urged my mother to go and find Beth. I did not know of this Messiah. I was just a boy. I was nine years old. I was just a boy …

"After this incident, my mother wished to go home, and argued with Joseph. Grandmother Beth intervened, suggesting that as all this nonsense was upsetting the children, perhaps it was best we go home. Her brother, Itharus, a short portly man, offered to take us home in his cart, while Joseph was left to journey on his own.

"Itharus had big brown eyes under bushy eyebrows, and was pleasant and good company, smiling whenever he looked at me, which was often. He stayed over, and after we had eaten, he took me for a walk.

"Holding my hand in his chubby fist, he asked me about any visions I had seen. He had this way about him, and I knew that I could tell him. I told him about the angel and the voices in my head. He looked into my eyes and when he said, 'You are blessed, and I believe you are the Son of our Father,' I believed him."

Jesus pauses, and I float into the group of men with whom Simeon had been standing. Images of the past overlapped one another in time with the beating of my heart.

Each member of the group greets a high priest by leaning forward and bowing. They touch the priest's right hand with one hand, and the other hand touches a scroll from the five books of Moses. The priest's beard is shaped and braided similar to a Persian king's. An argument draws my attention when a fisherman pays another priest with coins—his temple tax. One of Herod's soldiers stands and the argument subsides. A group of men stand tense and impatient, holding leather pouches of coins—a water carrier, a baker, a ferryman, a boat builder. A shepherd negotiates the price to be paid for a lamb. Priests bless young couples for marriage, while grooms' fathers negotiate the amount of temple tax to be paid.

Teased by the smell of wool and dung, memories of when I was a shepherd and shearer rise into my meditative state—and then Jesus continues.

"I feel you thinking of Rachael; it is because she is coming. She did not live in Joseph's home, and Joseph was cautious with his anger around Zebedee, so Rachael showed Joseph respect—until there was an unsettling event in her life. I do not know what happened to her—but this is not true. I will not share with you what happened to her. I will share that there was a hardening of her heart; no, that is not true either. Stillness crept over her, and for many months we did not play in the same way. In those times, when we went to our cave, there was a hunger and desperation about her.

"Things were happening to her that I did not understand; an urgency from her skin, her scent, and her touch. She let me touch her there, and it felt fresh. My entire body felt warm and alive, and I had an aching and hardness I had never before known. She let me lie on her, but I had no idea what I was doing—the fumbling of teenage innocence.

"Our childhood games had become more serious, and it frightened me. I was unnerved by how hungry she was. She touched herself, and then me, and I was nervous and wide-eyed—and then flushed and willing. When she cried out, I felt a release, there was wetness everywhere, and my whole body was quivering.

"We never went back to the cave after that, and were silent walking home. Something had come between us, but it had not been put there by our games; my father Joseph had put it there. Rachael will have the courage to tell you, Simon—in time.

"These are the stories that need to be written, because the Jesus you and your world know is a myth—He is a creation of the thoughts of man. I have always spoken to my Father, but I am in flesh. I am not God—I am in flesh."

Jesus leaves me exhausted. Close to collapse, I stumble wearily to bed. The residual emotion Jesus has left haunts me, and even though I'm exhausted, I'm having trouble falling asleep. Gegu holds my hand, and the last thing I remember is him telling me he loves me.

Trancing Jesus has made me remember how much Judas loved him, how much I loved him. It's difficult being the betrayer, and from the sorrow of my soul rises my nemesis—the painful memories of Judas.

Jesus is bathing in the shallows of a stream, and I am reluctant to join him. Unable to disrobe or turn and flee, I can only admire the muscle tone and texture of my friend's skin. The cool air has seduced his nipples, and my eyelids fall, heavy with desire. Sun-warmed air fills my chest, and my lashes float upwards. Droplets of water hang from his soft stomach hair, teased erect by a gentle breeze. One droplet hypnotizes me as it negotiates his abdominal muscles with increasing speed, undulating towards his genitals.

My hands cease shaking when Jesus takes them in his. He helps me to undress as if I am a child, and leads me into the water. Using a soft cloth, he washes the dust and stale sweat from my chest and back. His hands pause on each of the raised scars that are as numerous as animal tracks at a waterhole.

No part of my body is free from scarring. My father, in drunken rages, whipped me until my skin lacerated and burnt me with a red-hot iron rod. Sausage-shaped burn marks lie along my forearms and thighs in military precision. Ugly raised scars crisscross my torso and back and disrupt the order of the brands. Growing up, pain was my companion.

Unconcerned with our nakedness, Jesus embraces me and tells me he loves me. The feeling of his hips against mine overwhelm me and confused memories surface: my mother is moaning and encouraging men to fill her, while fat, groping fingers crawl over my skin like bed lice looking for the tastiest bite.

Jesus uncovers all my pain, and cleanses me with his embrace. In time, I'm able to look into his eyes, and for the first time in my life, I am loved— Judas is loved. Why am I the betrayer?

RACHAEL

For a while, I thought I had lost the tape that contained this trance, and then I worried about whether or not I had taped over it. I ring Max and Janu, and they tell me I still have it, so I rummage through my tapes again, and the first tape I put my hand on is the one I am looking for.

Gegu is smiling at me, and finally I hear him clearly. He had been trying to tell me where the tape was, but because of my worried state, I was unable to hear him.

The more frustrated I get the harder it is for me to hear spirit. I must be relaxed to communicate with spirit. Gegu has taught me my mind must be calm to receive the voices of spirit. Joanne's guide, Miriam, calls this, "the easy mind". Gegu calls it, "the path of no path".

I hear spirit through the base of my skull, and it is not like hearing naturally. I believe a person's thinking voice is often their guide's voice, and as they fine-tune their connection with spirit, the voice will gradually adopt its own accent and personality.

Rachael introduced herself on November 6, 2000. She is a little taller than her mother, but her confident stance makes her appear much taller. She has mischievous eyes with beautiful, long eyelashes. Her cheeks are full and rosy and her hair is curly and out of control. Although she seems like a bit of a tomboy, she is striking. She looks like an athlete, muscular and solid, without any fat. She has a funny way of tilting her head to the side, and when she puts her hands on her hips, she looks like a tempestuous child, but when she smiles, she just looks cheeky. Now she smiles and winks. I have kept her waiting long enough.

Rachael

"Hello, Simon. I have been waiting patiently to speak to you; it's exciting to share my life with you.

"Although my mother gave me to Miriam to look after, they raised all the children together. The only children they had no control of were the boys. Once they went fishing with Zebedee, they were lost to their mothers; that was Zebedee's way.

"Miriam breast-fed James and me together, and we have always had a good relationship. James broke Zebedee's heart when he left with John and travelled with Jesus. James's faith was strong, and Zebedee, who could foresee the outcome of James's actions, was fearful for his son's life, but I also wondered if he was a bit jealous, too.

"Zebedee showed his love by working his sons hard. When James was growing up, he had high hopes for him. It wasn't that he needed him to fish, because by this time he had a large fleet of fishing boats. He showed love to his sons by working with them, and when they were gone, he found it hard to fill this space in his life. He was burdened by the loss of Michael, Joachim, and Anna's boy. I think when John and James left, he felt that loss again.

"Joachim and Anna, Joseph and Mary and their children lived in a three-room dwelling. Extending out the back was a stable area and courtyard with a low rock wall on either side. Zebedee and Miriam also lived in a three-room dwelling; the mirror image of Joseph and Mary's. The courtyard wall connected the two homes. The stable area was on Zebedee and Miriam's side of the courtyard. If you looked out Joseph and Mary's back door, the stable was on the right and the yard area in between. There was a storage bin attached to the house, beneath the stable roof, and the yard was often filled with ducks and geese. Anna used their eggs for baking.

"When Jesus arrived home after his birth, I was only three years old and I don't recall the event. Miriam kept me away because Mary was tired from the journey, and the pregnancy had strained her.

"And so I got to play with baby Jesus in my fourth year. It's not that we never had anything to do with each other; it was just that I was too loud and rough, so I was prevented from getting under Mary's feet.

"Jesus had a funny way of crawling, which used to make me laugh. I would try to get him to stand, but he was happy crawling. When he finally got to his feet, I'd hold his hands and help him walk. As we grew up, I'd often look over to Mother Mary's place and give him a wave.

"If Zebedee was home, we'd always have our meals with him, but if he was still out at sea, we ate with Grandmother Anna and Mary.

"My mother Miriam was handy with a needle and thread. She was a seamstress of sorts and mended clothing for people. It was a good community, and skills and goods were traded freely.

"I remember the trip to Lazarus', but I couldn't see what all the fuss was about; the tears and everything. Jesus was always crying, and I would look at him, shake my head and rough him up a bit.

"We did have chores to do; we had to sweep the yard, tend the animals, carry goods to market, help my mother with her sewing, and we had clothing to wash, but because so many people lived in our homes, everything got done quickly.

"Zebedee was my father, but I did look to Joseph whenever he was home. I didn't like the constant bickering or his shifting moods, but it was his home, not mine, and I respected him because I knew he was my real father, so whenever he was in a good mood, I tried to spend time with him.

"Jesus has shared the story of our hidey hole, and whenever we could get away, we spent time there together. I was three years older than he, so I went through puberty before he did, and I often encouraged him to touch my breasts and pubic hair. During our games in the cave, I was the bossy one. I'd make Jesus get his penis out and then I would touch it. He was always keen to get his clothes off, but that is the way of boys, and then we would lie together, pretending we were grownups.

"I remember the beating he got from Joseph. I saw him the next day, and we went down to the beach for a swim, and I bathed his bruises. He was withdrawn for a couple of weeks afterwards. It upset me to see him like that.

"Jesus and I often went to the markets together and met the other boys and girls of the village at the well. It was there I befriend Elizabeth, who was visiting family in Nazareth. She was six or eight months older than me, and was the only other person we took to our hiding place. I dared Jesus to kiss her, and when he did, I felt a little bit jealous, which was silly, because Elizabeth was good company.

"Jesus and I continued to go to the cave until he was eleven and I was fourteen. I was at the age where I had learned to touch myself, squeezing my thighs together and enjoying the sensations that produced, in the way of teenage girls. One day, I went to the cave with young Jesus. We took off our clothes and lay together, and I got him to touch me where it felt the best. It was exciting, different from when I did it, and so I held him, rubbed him against me—he was shy and innocent—then guided his hand to touch me again and suddenly, wetness spurted from his penis. He was sensitive to touch afterwards, which made us laugh. It was funny but brought shyness between us, and this would be the last time we went to the cave together.

"I am not embarrassed to be telling you this story, for I was always the ringleader, and have always been the cheeky one in the family. These are important stories that need to be told, so you can all see that Jesus was just like any other boy; for all Jesus' gifts, he was still only a boy.

"I knew that Jesus was different, however, and I knew he was going to go away. I knew it before he left, and when he did, I missed him an awful lot.

"I will come and speak to you again. Thank you for listening to me."

Rachael spoke candidly about her life, and she wasn't reserved when sharing her maturing sexual desires. Aware that I was experiencing all she was describing, Rachael guided me gently through her puberty. It's harder editing her transcript than it was trancing with her. Being a father of girls, I feel uncomfortable hearing about a teenage girl's blossoming sexuality. During trance I become Rachael, and Simon the father is separated from the experience.

Rachael is cute, but her confidence hasn't fooled me. We don't hug when I type the account of her trance, but rather lean against each other for comfort, and even though she tries to hide it I'm aware of her soft nature.

Thank you, Rachael, and I love your curls. She smiles and swings her hips cheekily as she walks away.

The next day, November 7, 2000, Rachael returns. After my trance with Jesus, I knew Rachael would come to speak with me again.

Rachael

"Hello again, Simon. It was Zebedee with whom I had the greatest bond. He was my father, the one who held my cheeks and wiped my tears whenever I cried. He always had time and kind words for me, and he made me feel as important as his boys.

"But I still loved and respected Joseph, my real father. I enjoyed seeing him when he was home, and I enjoyed helping him. Sometimes he'd let me carry his tools, and little things like that made me happy.

"Then, one day when I was twelve, Joseph was to travel to Bethlehem to do some work for the Magdalene's He offered to take me with the boys, James and Jude. I was excited to be able to talk to him away from everyone else, and he was attentive when we camped for the night on our way to Bethlehem. I was enjoying the adventure of being away from home, and I was pleased to serve Joseph, away from the bustle of our families.

"While we were in Bethlehem, we ate lunch at a teahouse, and I watched Joseph smiling at the young lady who served him. I wondered at this; the look in his eyes, and the way she reacted to him, allowing him to gaze upon her breasts. Now that I am an adult, I look back and realize that she had stirred him, but had given him no release.

"On the road home, Joseph took to drinking. When we settled for the night, he was quite merry. After we had eaten supper, the two boys went to sleep under the cart, lying back to back for comfort and warmth, while Joseph and I slept under the awning near the fire.

"This was my first trip away with Joseph and I was enjoying his company. I was content when he pulled me closer; it was rare that he held me thus. His hands settled on my bottom and breasts, but I thought nothing of it. He was talking softly, telling me I was special, and I believed him. He said he wished to feel my warmth, and snaked his hand under my robe. I was too scared to move. I knew it was wrong, but I trusted him, and looked up to him.

"I could feel him moving behind me, a rhythmic movement as he held my breasts, first one and then the other. Then his hand snaked lower, but I was too respectful to pull away. He found my warm spot, and what he was doing didn't hurt; I was very confused. Then, he asked me to watch what he was doing. He had it in his hand. I had seen one before, but not like this. I had seen my brothers passing their morning water, but I hadn't seen one like this before. This was nothing like my games with Jesus.

"He kept one hand on me, pushing harder, rubbing, and then he asked for my hand. He said it would be all right, and he wouldn't tell anyone. He grabbed my hand and placed it on his thing. It was hot, and he moved my hand up and down. Soon, he started to make a funny noise, and then he shuddered and there was wetness on me. I was dazed, and felt ashamed, although I didn't know what I had done wrong, for Joseph fell asleep without talking to me. It had gone all soft and little, and I pulled my hand away, trying not to wake him. Drawing my legs up close to my stomach, I rocked myself to sleep. I never said anything to anyone about what had happened.

"The first night home I cried and cried, and when Zebedee came to soothe me I yelled harsh words at him and hurt his heart. I did not mean to upset Zebedee, but I overheard him talking to Miriam and knew there was now a divide between Zebedee and me, which he did not deserve. I never held my father Joseph again."

After this, I am feeling distressed and embarrassed, and I can see Rachael being comforted by Jesus. I had suspected what Rachael was going to say, but I wasn't prepared for the impact it would have on me. Now I feel lonely and indecisive. I feel like washing my hands.

While in trance I experience what it was like for Rachael to lose her innocence. Her happiness from being with Joseph was crushed. In her confusion she thought she had disappointed him, and this was why he fell asleep without saying goodnight. While Joseph's ejaculate cooled on her hand, she was waiting for him to wake up and wash her hands and tell her he loved her.

This episode accelerated Rachael's blooming sexuality, and brought new urgency to her games with Jesus. Her experience altered the way she thought about the other men in her family, and caused disquiet between her and Zebedee.

In my life I am close to only a handful of people. I tell those people I love them, and I mean it—not the romantic love I have for Joanne, but the love of respect, admiration and compassion. I have grown to love Jesus' family. I feel protective of them, and I also feel responsible that they are reliving such painful moments in their lives again.

On December 25, 2000, I stay up late to proofread this manuscript, and Rachael arrives.

"Hello, Simon." She is shy and subdued.

"Hello, Rachael. How are you?"

"Oh … I'm sorry for putting you through that."

I know she is referring to the emotions I experienced during our trance. She leans against me, and drapes an arm around my shoulders.

"Hey, are you okay?" I ask.

"No," she replies in the tiniest voice. The voice might be tiny, but it's wielding a hammer, and crushes my heart. I sigh and tell her I love her. Rachael climbs into my lap, and starts to cry. I hold her and rock her gently. She stays in my lap for a long time. I can feel her. She is real.

MY FAMILY

My stepson Scott is almost four years old, and is able to see spirit the same way Max sees spirit: as colored, shimmering forms of energy. Scott's a big boy: barrel-chested, soft-bellied, fence posts for thighs, and he has a beach-ball shaped face. He likes monster-trucks, motorbikes, roast dinners, and sleepovers at Joanne's sister's place. Joanne clips his sun bleached hair short for summer, and this makes his round cheeks and smile seem even bigger. He tans Australian surfer-boy gold, which makes his perfect white teeth look even brighter. He has gentle hands and an innate kindness.

Scott is on the bed with Joanne and me when he asks excitedly, "Where is that green light coming from?" He stands up and peers at the wall, and when he changes position, he loses sight of the green light. "Where's it gone Mum? There it is!" he says, excited once again.

Joanne and I cannot see the light, but Miriam and Gegu are telling us it is Miriam giving Joanne some healing. Scott, standing now, is still looking. "Oh, I must have scared it away." Smiling, he bounces on the bed while looking for his elusive light. This happens again the next day in the lounge. This time the light is on the ceiling, and the colors he sees are blue and purple. I'm certain Scott doesn't think the colors he sees are spirit.

Scott is easily distracted. If he's not getting all the attention, he becomes loud and obtrusive: he fights with his sister, argues with his mother, and gets sent to his room by two fathers.

His room is always a hive of spirit activity. When I walk into his room, I walk through his guide who is standing in the doorway. At home, spirits get my attention in one of three places: the kitchen, the shower, or outside Scott's room. When I kiss Scott goodnight I always talk to Tachi, his main guide.

Tachi is tall for a Japanese person. He's fit and muscular with a dark complexion. He loves to smile, has a good sense of humor and his warrior's topknot is plaited with a golden thread. He was born in 1563 on the island of Kyushu, and after the execution of his parents, was raised as a warrior monk in a Zen monastery. He later became a bodyguard and personal trainer to a prince and his family. The love they shared grew, and Tachi was adopted as a son.

I asked Tachi if he would like to be in this book, and he was excited to have the opportunity to speak. This is the conversation I had with him when I looked in on Scott at 2 AM.

"How is he?"

"He is fine, my lord."

"Is it you I walk through every night?"

"Hai."

"How many of you watch over my son?"

"There are many of us."

As I heard his answer, Gegu whispered "Eight."

"That is an awful lot of protection for the little man."

"He is gifted, and he must be protected. In time he will use this gift, but he must endure an emotional life first, similar to the path you have travelled."

"Do you wish to share your life with me so I may write about it?"

"Hai. I would be honored, my lord."

Tachi insisted on addressing me as "my lord" and I wondered why, but the answer was right under my nose. In his lifetime I had been the prince he had served. Scott's sister, Lee, had been my concubine, and was escorted by

Tachi and his fellow brother monk Hiro, whom Scott had been. Tachi and Hiro had both been orphaned by the wars of feuding clans and had grown up together.

The prince's son, my son, had been placed in Hiro's care. My son died falling from a horse, and even though I was forgiving, Hiro took his own life; it was the honorable thing to do. Tachi was his second, and beheaded Hiro after he had completed the abdominal cut. Tachi is showing me all of this as he watches me type.

"Once again I am beside my brother, and when he passes into rebirth I will aid him again."

Tachi rests on his knees with his hand on the hilt of his sword. He is on my left side, and Gegu is on my right. Tachi is a master swordsman and sensei of many Japanese weapons and karate. When I first became aware of Tachi, I used to address him as sensei, but he did not wish to be called sensei; he only wanted to come to karate and train with me. Recently, I closed my karate club, and Tachi was disappointed because he had offered to help me train.

As easily as I can trance spirit, I am able to use Tachi to guide my body through martial arts training—or so he tells me. "Faith," whispers Gegu.

"Tachi?"

"Yes, my lord," he replies, bowing respectfully.

"Do you wish to share some wisdom with us?"

"Hai. A flower does not bloom to show off to its neighbors. It blooms so it may bloom again the following spring.

"We are petals on the one bloom, but we are most beautiful when we return to the earth to feed the new blooms of another spring."

"Thank you, Tachi."

"My lord."

"Simon. Please call me Simon."

"Yes, my lord."

Tachi bows and moves to stand in Scott's doorway. His philosophies are as ambiguous as Gegu's, and I like the way they both speak because they challenge me to think. Tachi is an angel and he is a member of my family. Every night I bid him goodnight, I sleep a little easier knowing he is watching over Scott.

Tachi was grinning when he walked away; he found my request, for him to call me Simon, funny. I'm always asking him to call me Simon, and his response is always the same.

When Tachi is close to me, I feel confident, and when he's not making me smile, I feel almost in awe of him. I'm not easily impressed. I have never been a celebrity junkie, but I admire intelligence, compassion and sporting ability, and Tachi has all of those qualities. I feel like I'm the one who should be calling him, "my lord".

Scott's sister, Lee, is wise beyond her six years. Her personality is similar to her mother's, so they butt heads regularly and disrupt the household.

Lee, like her mother, looks you in the eye when she speaks to you. She's intelligent, reads above her age and questions every instruction her mother gives her. Joanne doesn't like being told how to do something by a six year old. Lee likes to be in control.

This is a no win situation for a tired tradesman. Do I chastise Lee for being right—undermining her confidence and Joanne's authority—or remain silent? Lee, with all her stubbornness, is still lovely, and is interested when I'm working with spirit. She knows that when I'm at the computer I'm not talking to myself, and she asks whom I'm speaking to.

Lee is a talented artist, and has been drawing since she was two years old. Her artwork is mature and rich with detail; I know she has a guide that helps her draw. His name is Louis; he is French, and he lived in the fifteenth century. In his lifetime, Lee was his sister Marie, who died in her early twenties, from pneumonia. Louis' favorite moments were spent with his sister, picnicking and painting landscapes together. Lee is unaware she has help to draw, but Louis assures me they spend time together when Lee is sleeping.

Lee's main guide is Tu-tau, and I apologize to him if I have misspelt his name. Tu-tau is a Tibetan farmer from the twelfth century, and is an herbalist and a healer. He knows about acupuncture and bone setting and tells me that an old grandfather, who adopted him after he was orphaned, trained him in these arts. Lee was his sister, who was crippled and disfigured in a landslide. Tu-tau nursed her for many years but she "passed away to the clouds."

"Thank you, Tu-tau."

"You are welcome, keeper."

"Gegu?"

"Yes, my son. He calls you keeper; you keep his little sister, and this makes him happy. He knows that one day you will guide her to him."

When Tu-tau is close to me I feel earthy. When I breathe in, the rainforest glides by.

Tu-tau smells like honey and pepper. He walks hunched over and supports himself with a walking stick. When he brushes against me I feel alert, and I can hear insects and frogs. He enjoys every sound he hears and the scents of his mountain retreat. He makes me feel happy: I am almost smiling in sleepy contentment.

"Keeper of my princess and savior of children; I see you, young one.

"If it does not rain in the forest then the orchids will not bloom, and if the orchids do not bloom then the bees will not come. If the bees do not come then how will the orchids be pollinated to start the circle of life? Was it the orchid first or the bee? Why seek an answer when one cannot be found?

"Why lift a rock to see what is underneath when the rock is already happy, and do we even care if the rock is happy? To live, we must eat, and to eat we must harvest, and if we must harvest then we must care for our lands. How many rocks will we need to move to feed our families? And when we have exhausted our lands, who will put the rocks back?

"How is it we can climb to the moon, and yet we are unable to walk into our fields and return them to the mother? And if we are careless with our mother, how can we raise our children? All the medicines we need are kept in the forests, and if we take them and do not replace them, how will we live?

"My princess is only dust in the Universe, but if she is removed, is the Universe less or more? A king was sent and you write his story, but is he more than my princess, more than dust?

"A king was taken from his mother and a sickness spread which has affected all who are cowards in the shadow of the Mother. It has happened time and time again. Soon it will be too late for our fields, and so it will be too late for our children. Your fields are your homes, and the rocks you have removed are the charity of an innocent heart, and your children are born into heartless homes ...

"Oh, you pretend to live with love, naturally, until you look to your neighbor and wish to be better than he; his skin is a different shade, his language you do not speak, his place of worship is less regal, and what you imagine he has is not worthy of his ownership.

"Is one grain of dust bigger than the Universe? Only if you wish it to be, only if you believe it to be so, and mayhap your home is not lost. My princess is dust and she is seen by God. How many times have you overlooked dust?"

I feel blessed that I'm able to speak to Gegu and the other angelic guides in my family because they have made me a better person, a better father and a better partner. But my life is far from easy. I experience emotional tragedy on a regular basis.

During the months of trancing with Jesus and his family, Joanne lost our child at seven weeks. We knew our child would be a boy, because Gegu,

Miriam, and Ruth, had told us. Even though his flesh has gone, with Gegu's counsel, I know his spirit remains.

I was given no warning that we'd lose our son, but there's a small, bright light that flicks in and out of my sight, and I know this is my son. He will continue to grow with Joanne and me, and when we pass over he will be there to greet us. I'm sure we will both speak to him well before then. My son will lie in Gegu and Miriam's arms and, if I try, I will feel him in mine.

The wonder of it is that I don't need to feel him to know he is there. That is faith, and that is something Gegu has taught me. I *know* my son is with me.

Joanne cried in private, and I just cried. Tears are the best healers of all, because healing is the release of pain. Gegu must have thought Joanne had not cried enough, because he prompted me to leave a scrolling message on her screensaver.

"Hello, Mother. I am not too far away. If you close your eyes I will lie on your chest and listen to your heartbeat again."

Joanne cried and pretended to dislike us, but we knew different. A few days later I tranced Gegu for her, and he talked about our son, who was now in his care. Joanne's guide, Miriam, will continue to carry the child to full term. If Joanne wishes, she can visit Miriam in the field where they often meet and share in the pregnancy. If Joanne wants, she can be present at the birth and be Miriam's midwife. Together, Gegu and Miriam will raise our son, and he will grow like any other child.

Some spiritualists might question whether this message from Gegu is symbolic, and suggest that it is for healing, and not to be taken literally. I believe some spirits of children grow into adults in the place to which their energy has passed.

Five years after this loss a young boy materialized beside me while I was driving. He looked like a photograph of me when I was five. I turned my head. He didn't disappear. He smiled.

"Hello dad."

I cried.

"It's okay dad. I love you."

Joanne's sister, Belinda, gave birth to a stillborn baby boy, and whenever I was around Belinda, a spirit boy used to get my attention and say, "Hello, Uncle Simon. Tell Mummy I love her." The boy was the right age to be Tommy if he had lived. He looked like his brother, and I used to watch him play with his brother and sister when I visited.

To help Belinda with her grieving, I discussed this with her and suggested we meditate together and I'd attempt to introduce her to Tommy. My idea was that we would meditate at the same time, but I would meditate at home and she would meditate at her place, ten kilometers away.

In my meditation, I walked into a field of grass and daisies and saw Belinda sitting near a tree. Tommy walked towards Belinda and sat with her, but at this stage I had to stop meditating because I was a sobbing mess. I believe I was experiencing the grief that Belinda was unable to let go of.

The next day, Belinda phoned me and described, without any input from me, the exact same location and events I had seen, and told me that after I had left the meditation, Tommy sat in her lap and told her he loved her. Belinda also said she had "a good cry," which I had experienced.

Now, either I have superhuman powers of mind manipulation that are effective up to ten kilometers away, or the place in which Belinda talked to Tommy is real. This was the first and only time I have done this, and Gegu had prompted me to suggest it to Belinda.

To all those parents who have lost children, particularly mothers who have lost a baby, I hope I can comfort you by saying that I believe your children are alive and well, and they are still close to you, because your guides are close to you.

My extended family is growing day by day, and I am thankful for my gift. It's important to realize we can all communicate with spirit; if we only choose to.

It's late, and I was going to end this chapter here, when Julie—a spirit who lives with us—said, "Don't forget me."

"How can I, when you are always under my feet? Now, off to bed with you."

Julie runs to join Joanne in bed, and I hear giggles and the padding of feet. When I pull the covers back to get into bed, Julie is lying on my side, so I ask her to move over. She smiles and appears to float across Joanne. When I snuggle up to Joanne, Julie floats back over us, lies behind me, and drapes her arm around me.

"Goodnight, Julie. I love you."

"I love you too."

DAVID AND THE SAVIOR

There's a difference between what I see in a meditative state and what I see day-to-day, and depending on what I'm doing, there are differences between meditations. It's like the difference between looking at a scene through the viewer of a digital camcorder and looking at the scene itself.

Imagine if you fell asleep on a bus in the city and woke up to find yourself traveling through a rainforest, when you had intended to get off the bus outside your home in the suburbs. You ask the bus driver, who is a close friend, if he will be returning to the city. He assures you he will, so you go back to sleep. When you arrive, you are in such a deep sleep the bus driver cannot wake you, so he carries you off the bus and into your home.

When you wake up, you tell your flat-mate about the magnificent rainforest you saw, but he doesn't believe you. You didn't take a photo, nor did you get out of the bus and collect foliage. Your bus driver friend has left the country and was never introduced to your flat-mate, so you've got no hope of convincing your flat-mate that it actually happened.

You saw everything through a bus window, which is not the same as looking at it from outside the bus. Was the rainforest real? Did it really happen? You can't prove it because the only other person on the bus has disappeared. All your friends travel by bus, and no one has ever taken the scenic route through the rainforest, so some of your friends start to think it never happened; they start to question your sanity. Welcome to my world.

My spiritual development with Gegu and Jesus has taken place at supersonic speed. I don't know why, and I can't explain the science or the mechanics of the process. I don't clutter my experiences with too many questions; I only participate and observe. This may be the secret.

I feel spirits psychically, but I also feel them physically. I've already described the process of hearing spirit, but I can also smell and feel them. They embrace me, walk past and bump into me. I've been slapped on the ass and kissed on the cheek. I also experience these sensations during meditation.

Some of my meditations are symbolic. The images I see are random, and like computer generated images in a movie, they look artificial. I'm to interpret the vision rather than believe it to be real. If I see a winged horse, spirit is reminding me to soar. Still, reflective water means peace. A white dove is freedom, and a glowing hand reminds me that spirit is here to guide me.

In these meditations what I see is dreamlike, but in other meditations I have out-of-body experiences and go *somewhere*. It's easy for me to believe the *somewhere* I go is real, because occasionally I have returned from those places bruised. I've been stabbed and have stabbed someone. Opening my eyes afterwards, the weight of the knife has startled me and I've dropped the blade, which has hit the floor then bounced away. The noise was real. The knife was visible. My eyes were open.

Having participated in martial arts and kickboxing for fourteen years, and spent many nights sparring for up to two hours, the feeling I get when I wake up the morning after an out-of-body experience is the same feeling I have when recovering from some of those sessions.

To help me understand the places I go during meditation, Gegu has described these worlds as part of an infinite onion, where each ring of the onion is another world. My spirit is able to travel to these places because the energy transfers effortlessly from one world to the next. Gegu assists in this transition, although he can't always come with me. In those situations, I'm Captain Kirk from *Star Trek*, and he's Scotty. Beam me up, Gegu.

Gegu has told me that twenty-four of these worlds co-exist with Earth. The borders of these realms cross over and intertwine the same way he has described the vibration of our individual spirits dripping into the infinite pool.

I know some people will consider this science fiction, and I respect that, but because I've experienced this first-hand, I believe it to be real. Gegu is my bus driver—he hasn't left the country—and this book is my photo album, filled with my holiday snaps.

When Jesus blessed me in my kitchen, all the children who came with him stayed, and whenever I think about them, I can see them moving around me. My backyard dissolves and becomes the valley in which they've set up camp. With meditation, I visit them. The children greet me by name. They start to call me Simon the savior, and ask if I'm the one who saves children. I have no idea what they're talking about.

One night, while I'm driving home from church with Joanne, I feel someone in the car with us. I ask Joanne to drive, and when I close my eyes, Gegu introduces me to Billy.

Billy is six years old and has drowned. He is unable to go through the light, so I leave my body and go to him. We are standing on the beach where he lost his life. He is holding a teddy bear. I crouch in front of him and ask what he is doing. He cradles his bear in his arms and says, "I can't find my mum and dad."

"It's okay, Billy. We'll find them."

Gegu is telling me his parents are fine, and that Billy has been dead for several months.

Billy looks surprised that I know his name, but he doesn't seem afraid. Behind him, I can see a pirate, and I ask Gegu who it is.

"It is his guide. Billy calls him The Captain. This is his imaginary friend."

Other spiritualists who do rescue work have told me that guides don't accompany lost spirits, but I haven't always found this to be the case with children. Children's guides often accompany them, and it's these spirits who direct the children to me. Trauma and fear prevent these children from finding the light without guidance from someone who is still living.

Gegu has shown me Billy's drowning, introduced me to his guide, and told me what to say to Billy.

"Hey, Billy, can I hold your bear?"

"No."

"That's a shame. Who is this pirate with you?"

"He's The Captain." Billy is confident with his answer, and his pirate grins and draws his sword.

"Well, what good is a pirate without a ship? Let's find some gold and string up some landlubbers."

Billy smiles and his pirate dances a jig, while behind Billy a pirate ship materializes, and a long boat is lowered and rowed to shore. When it reaches the beach, several mean-looking pirates, waving cutlasses, leap out of the boat and surround Billy. Brandishing a sword, Billy orders them to row him to his ship.

The whole scene fades and is replaced by a bright light, and I can hear Billy laughing while his pirate ship sails away on a golden ray, leaving me standing with The Captain, who shakes my hand solemnly then turns into light. This whole episode only takes a few minutes, and I know what I have done. I've sent a spirit to the light, but I never expected it to be this easy.

Billy returned one month later, and this time he gave me the bear. He thanked me and said he would like to visit again. For weeks afterwards spirits visited and asked me, "Are you the one who saves children?"

I ended up saving lots of children. Billy was the first, and the easiest, because I didn't have to replace broken limbs, rebuild burnt flesh, overcome the horror of being beaten to death by an abusive father, or thrown from a window by a depressed mother. I didn't have to die in a car crash because of a drunken driver, or be locked in a cupboard and die of fright after being sexually abused so badly I lost consciousness.

Gegu brought spirit after spirit to me, and I experienced all of their deaths—some traumatic, some senseless—all of them sad. Why?

"Because you have been chosen, my son."

Chosen?

Each time I walked these children to the light, I realized the same woman waited to greet them. The light was too bright for me to see her clearly, and Gegu wouldn't let me step closer, but I recognized her voice each time she said, "Thank you."

The rescue that saddened me the most was Julie. Julie is a spirit who hitched a ride home with Joanne and I one night after church. She liked Joanne, and would often hide little things that belonged to her, like nail scissors and pens. Joanne would stare at the spot where she had left something, walk from the room frustrated and return to find the object was back. Joanne always knew it was Julie. One night, to get Joanne's attention, Julie brushed against a pot plant and made it move. When Joanne said, "Hello Julie," the pot plant stopped moving.

When we went to kiss Scott and Lee goodnight, Julie would be waiting for her kiss. She talked to me daily. Both Joanne and Max had seen the hem of her dress moving down the hallway, and I had seen her in the flesh, walking beside Joanne. She looked up, smiled and waved. This went on for many months, and I grew to love her like my own daughters. But the day came when I had to say goodbye.

My relationship with Julie grew because she loved me with every particle of her being. She didn't react if I was dirty and sweaty, and the expression in her eyes didn't change even if I was in a bad mood. Truth was, she improved my mood.

Spirits don't encroach on your privacy or your intimacy. They're present, but remain unaffected by nudity. I mention this because of the location Julie chose for me to lead her to the light. She chose the shower because this is where I'm most relaxed. My mind is still, my body is calm, and that is what was needed for me to say goodbye.

I'd been in the shower for a few minutes when Julie asked if she could bathe with me. Smiling, she materialized out of the steam and I invited her in. When she took off her white dress, I could see our beautiful Julie was scorched black by the fire that had taken her life. I realized she was here to be rescued. The tears welled up inside me when she stepped into the shower, and I relived the horror of her death. I became Julie, burning and dying: I was spared no detail.

While my heart broke, I bathed Julie with a golden balm. As my hands glided across the field of scorching pain, her charcoaled body was restored to its youthful beauty, and my tears washed away the golden soapsuds. Crouching down, I said to her, "Darling I didn't know." I kissed her sad eyes, held her hand and waited. Soon, an angel came for her from the ceiling—a solar-charged teardrop with eyes—and my Julie was gone, swallowed by the light. A piece of my heart went with her. It was too hard. I lay my head against Gegu's chest. Then, the angel reappeared.

"My name is Celeste, and I am the one who meets the children. I am the keeper of their precious souls and I have sent all the children who have come to you. You are their savior, and our Father needs you to go to another place. You must not be afraid; I will be waiting for you."

The light around her was so bright that I was unable to see her clearly. When she was gone, my heart felt like it was breaking again.

Julie returned some months later, having chosen to spend this lifetime with us. I am forever grateful to the Universe for the love with which she fills my home.

I ask Gegu about this place I need to go to, and he replies, "You have already been there." In recent meditations, I visited a valley and watched children playing in fields of daisies. Occasionally, a child would be sitting alone and I'd sit with him and encourage him to play, but I never thought to lead any of the children along the pathway. The valley looked like a happy place: bright, sunny, the grass green, the flowers fragrant, with multi-colored butterflies, and birds flying and chirping. I didn't understand why I would be afraid until I asked Gegu.

"This is a nowhere place—a place of fear and darkness. The souls here are lost, trapped in this dimension by the horrors of their deaths. Every soul here belongs to a child, and they are prey; this is the domain of the opposite one. It is you who brings the light to this place."

"The opposite one?"

"Yes, my son: Lucifer."

Now hang on a minute. I don't think hell or the devil is real, but I'd noticed that some angels don't seem to have our best interests at heart. Are these forces combative, in an eternal struggle to steal our souls? Curiously, Gegu remains quiet. His choice of words intrigued me, and I assumed he meant Lucifer preyed on young souls, but I was mistaken.

The name Lucifer is as foreign to my lips as cigarette butts, speaking in tongues and singing Celine Dion songs. What name would I have spoken if I was born in a Muslim country, in India, or China? The end of days champion doesn't visit my dreams or frequent my imagination, but if I'm to trust Gegu, and I must, he's as real as all the other angels that visit.

Previously, Jesus had a conversation with me about the angel Beelzebub; this was the *demon* he'd encountered at the market as a boy. He'd also used the name Lucifer during that conversation, but he'd not forewarned of this moment.

Some years later, I learn that it's not Lucifer who is combative, but the energy of human consciousness that has pooled in these places. Lucifer is not the hunter; he is the light. The energy forms a prison. Lucifer is dark, because he swims in *oil*.

If I had been asked during a meditation, I may have thought it was symbolic, but since a glowing phantom had materialized in my bathroom and asked, I knew this was real. And you know, the funny thing was, I said, "Hey, let's go." Gegu just smiled.

Before I go any further, I need to share two things that happened to me at the time I started to visit the valley. The first was a meditation where I visited another world and met with a … let's call him a galactic general. This warrior's name was Hazabar, and he gave me an army of what I call man-beasts; legions. When I emerged from my meditation, I brought this army with me, and if I close my eyes and ask Gegu to show them to me, they stretch from horizon to horizon.

Man-beasts stand over two and a quarter meters. Their upper body is broad and looks out of proportion with their legs. They hold their long arms slightly bent, and they stand leaning forward. Their jaws jut forward, and the color of their deep-set eyes is lighter than the shades of gold that shimmer across their flesh.

They surround me like well-paid bodyguards. When I look up, they come to attention and salute me with their lances. As this was the first time that a non-human spirit had followed me home, I questioned if they were real. Gegu smiled, and one of the giant, golden gladiators crouched down and rested his forehead against mine. He felt solid, and warm breath-like waves of energy blew into my face. I pushed forward, but I was unable to get up. The beast felt real. I felt peaceful.

These Golden Neanderthals don't need armor, as they're pure love, and they serve the Infinite pool. They're battle-hardened warrior angels from another world, and they now look after a plumber.

The other thing that had been happening was that every time I talked with Gegu, he would say, "Someone's coming."

"Who?" I'd ask.

"The general." I had no idea what Gegu was talking about, and then the king arrived.

Once again, I'm at my kitchen sink. The air is humming and I'm tingling from head to toe, like a mobile phone set to vibrate every time God calls. Suddenly, my kitchen disappears. It's like driving into the sun and the glare through the windscreen causes you to lose sight of the road until the angle of the windscreen changes. I close my eyes to protect them from the glare. When I open them again, I'm looking over a desert steppe.

In front of me, hordes of man-beasts close ranks and come to attention, while across the plain a dust cloud billows towards us. The pounding of running feet and the sound of blades against pumping thighs, of shields against shoulders, and the rhythmic symphony of adrenaline-charged breathing, rumble like thunder.

This advancing army stops and faces the ranks of man-beasts. A narrow corridor separates them. A man riding a white stallion canters towards me down the corridor. His army cheers and bang their swords against their shields, and the man-beasts drum the butts of their lances into the desert; and I know who he is. He is David, King of Israel.

Dreamlike, I walk across the dusty steppe towards the general and his army. The air is dry, dust billows and the ground vibrates beneath my feet. I stop in front of the horse and look into David's penetrating brown eyes. I know this man, and my eyes slowly close. When I open them again I'm on the horse, and my shoulders flex when I salute my army with a golden shield. The soldiers cheer, and with a burst of golden light I turn into an angel. The sun is shining from my chest. When I close my eyes the light fades and I'm back in my kitchen.

At no time did I consider these experiences weren't real. I was seeing ghostly other-world images, people and beings everywhere during my daily routine. I anticipated the arrival of Obi Wan Kenobi, "Use the force, Simon." Without humor I may have spiraled into madness.

With meditation, Max and I visit the valley again, together. Janu and Gegu cannot come because their vibrations will unbalance this place, but we're able to become our healing guides and bring some children back for Celeste.

I won't describe all the *battles* in this valley, but I will share the last of them. Max, Narelle, Anita, Sean and Stacey came with me into the valley. Everyone saw and experienced the same things: they each rescued children and fought demon-like creatures. None of them had seen a man-beast before, but everyone was able to describe what they looked like.

Trancing the Archangel David, I lead the meditation, and he leads us into the valley. But even I am surprised by what happens.

When David slips into my body, I feel calm. David's energy field is immense, and I feel like I'm expanding. During these experiences, my perception of the physical aspects of my body shift—I'm pliable, not solid. I'm connected to everything and nothing. The transformation is accompanied by a popping sound and I think about bubble wrap.

The darkness in front of my closed eyes disappears, and I am standing at the entrance to the valley. My healing guide is standing beside me, his loincloth moving with the breeze. His brown eyes meet mine, and he dips his head to let me know he's ready. The amber light highlights the muscles in his arm moving in time with the tomahawk he spins impatiently. Everyone else has become his or her healing guide, and Jesus has joined us. David speaks: "There is naught to fear here. The children here do not belong to the one who has fallen. He is my brother, torn from my chest, but he has no power against love, so love shall be your sword. He has no power against faith, so faith shall be your shield."

A part of my mind is observing this performance and I wonder why I sound like Charlton Heston from *The Ten Commandments*. It feels like Arnold Schwarzenegger has lent me his chest and shoulders, and my eyes scan the swirling darkness in front of us.

"A man-beast will guard your back, one will fight beside you, and another will take the children to Celeste."

Advancing with us is David's army, along with the legions of man-beasts. When we walk forward into the shadows, children rise from the ground, released from their graves by our passing feet. Man-beasts grasp the pitiful grey hands and pull the children free. Small mouths, desperate for air, gasp and gulp the golden mist that is rising from the beasts.

Some children, illuminated by the light that is moving forward with us, cower behind rocks and bushes, the talons of deformed banshees sunk into their flesh. It's like watching award-winning tattoos coming to life on under-age clients of Satan's tattoo emporium.

Inside a dark crevice, two red eyes lure me forward, and the golden flesh of the man-beast standing at my shoulder illuminates a huge serpent. Its coils are wrapped around a young girl; its curved fangs glisten with venom. With mongoose-like speed I charge into the crevice and turn the creature into smoky light. Like twirling patterns on volcanic glass, the serpent's scales dissolve into liquid light, and I pull the girl free.

Angels, materializing from the advancing light, tend to children and merge with the man-beasts. The dark breathes like a cancerous lung, sometimes ashen, then polished and flowing. From behind, the advancing man-beasts look like limbed comets. Filaments of light explore the dark, and children and demons tumble from the cracks.

Gliding forward, I face a squatting demon with too many arms, its body twisted grotesquely. Its fangs drip metallic saliva, and its clawed fingers tear at the flesh of a young boy. I reach for the boy with one hand and restore his flesh, while my other hand forms a fist that punches into the demon's chest. Tearing its soul free, I hand them both to a man-beast. The demon dissolves into light, and golden ash falls around us.

A dark angel, crouching on his haunches, watches without expression. His stillness is unnerving. Power radiates from him like fear from the terminally ill. The eyes, black and pupil-less, move like cooling lava. His wings seem to be coated with tar and the barbed hooks on his elbows complement the taloned fingers hanging between his bent knees.

His face is smooth and strong, and would look good on the big screen, but his energy belongs in a cruise missile. Dangerous. Malignant. This is Lucifer. I blink and I'm standing beside him. Placing a hand on his neck, I try to turn his face towards me.

"Will you not look me in the eye? Can you not be saved? This valley is no longer yours. These children return to our Father. Will you not join them?"

Without looking at me, Lucifer pulls away. The brightening atmosphere shimmers, and he's gone. Soldiers and man-beasts cheer, and I can see children being helped to their feet by light beings. The symphony shifts the energy and everyone returns to their body.

Walking up the path, Celeste embraces me and we become one—David and Celeste, super-angel. When I return to the room, everyone has a story to share. I look at Max, and he smiles.

I'm not sure how I was able to remain so relaxed about these experiences. I'd go to work to lay drains and brush against angels and man-beasts. The landscapes and beings from my meditations were materializing in the physical world. Angels appear in many cultures, but why was I seeing them now?

The chain of events had happened so quickly I didn't have time to think about what was happening. If what I was seeing had stayed in my mind, it may have driven me crazy. Did I question if this was real? Frequently. But every time I did, an angel appeared and physically interacted with me. Why was I having these experiences now, interspersed with the conversations with Jesus and family?

I sought Diane's opinion on the spirit rescues, and her response was, "It's not possible. You're too inexperienced." I wondered if there was a secret society of smoking, panty-less spirit rescuing spiritualists that I wasn't eligible to join. She then challenged me to tell her who her guide was as no one had ever identified her guide. I described him perfectly. She was shocked. I'd have thought she'd be happy. I felt disorientated. No one can explain what I'm going through.

The valley is a safe place now, and Celeste is able to walk the children to the light without my help. The valley is like a children's hospital that specializes in healing the spirits of children who died violent deaths: it's a special burns unit—grafting flesh before a child can be moved on to physiotherapy and recovery.

Returning often, I have walked many children towards the light. I cannot go into the light, but figures materialize and shake my hand; they embrace and kiss me and thank me for saving their children. Children walking into the light recognize their parents, relatives, and friends.

There is a lot I don't understand, but from Gegu I have learned there is *darkness* in the Universe, and man has created it. Every time we are violent, hate-filled, racist, scornful, envious, or experience any negative emotion, we create dark energy. It's the same as pouring oil into our oceans, and this oil, this energy, pools in consciousness and creates places like the valley. The darkness is not there to balance the light. It is there because we put it there.

Dark angels mean us no harm. The darkness in the valley is fear, created by the circumstances of each child's death. Once trapped, this energy self-evolves and remains in the energy field of the Earth.

We have created Lucifer—think of him as energy, only as energy, trapped between the physical Earth, and the infinite pool, the source: God. Humanity and the habits of history have built a weir, and our spirits cannot flow freely back to the infinite pool.

At times I wonder if everything I experience is from an interactive game console, a Play Station with angel-powered graphics. Am I Neo, the chosen one, or another insane gamer locked in a duel of biblical proportions with an anonymous gaming opponent—myself?

JAMES

On the November 8, 2000, Jesus introduces me to his brother James. The stubble on my lip curls into the dry corners of my mouth, and it feels like bindi seeds are playing hopscotch on my thighs. The sound of my neighbor's lawn mower chases me downstairs and I break my dog's heart as I hurry past. I slam the downstairs door too hard and sigh when I sit down. Gegu and James wait patiently for me to close my eyes.

I'm not sure what bothers me. I'm exhausted and looking for a fight. I fall asleep bathed in light.

James

"Hello, Simon. I never had an understanding of my brother Jesus. He was gentle and spent too much time with the women, and not enough time at work. Like most brothers, Jude and I were rivals, and we had many battles. We wrestled, we punched, we cheated and we lied, but not Jesus; if the blame was his, he took it.

"I saw the beating he got from our father Joseph, and I was frightened for him. I cannot remember if I had ever slept with him before, but on that night I came to him. He slept restlessly, which was often his way, but this time I sat beside him and stroked his sweat-soaked hair away from his forehead. I held his hands and marveled at their softness.

"His hands did not harden until he came and worked with stone, and that was a terrible four months for him during which time his hands were often bleeding. My brother's heart was always soft, and while his hands eventually hardened, his heart did not.

"When I was twelve and Jesus was fifteen, he wandered into the stable one day and found me throwing stones at a mouse. When he tried to intervene, I turned and shoved him, then picked up an even bigger stone and dropped it on the mouse. Tears welled up in his eyes, but even though he was crying, he was also strong. I had never seen him like this before.

"He grabbed me with his left hand and forced me to the ground then uncovered the mouse with his right hand. He bade me to look at it, which I did, and then with his right hand he placed my hand on the mouse so that I could feel the stickiness of the blood. I started to cry. Then I felt warmth such as I had never before felt.

"'Look what you have done. Now, look what I can do,' he said, and then, miraculously, he brought the mouse back to life. When he lifted my hand away, the mouse scurried off. I stared at Jesus in wonder. He stroked my cheek and looked into my heart, but said nothing and walked away from me.

"This unsettled me for many days, but as time went on, I held onto my resentment for him—resentment that he was not there to work, not there to share the burden of a father who cheated on our mother. Then, suddenly, he was gone. I was fourteen, I was bitter and I hated him.

"I moved on with my life after that. I moved away from Nazareth with my beautiful Sarah, who gave birth to three wonderful children. I moved to Bethlehem to work with wood and stone, to raise my children, and to love my Sarah, but I often heard the stories of this man who was my brother.

"I was not at his crucifixion, for I had turned away from my family, but I had heard of the murder. I went to visit my mother and look on my sweet sisters, who had had the foulest things done to them. Then, heavy with shame, I turned away from my sisters and returned to my Sarah and my life.

"I did see Jesus again, however, for he came to me one night when I was sick with pneumonia and shaking with fever. He came and held my hand and wiped my brow and spoke to me. "This is for the time when you came and tended me when our father had beaten me; this is the love I hold for you." Then, he was gone. In the morning I was well again.

"I wished I could have shown my love to him, the brother I had turned away from, but I was as selfish as my father."

James is a private person, and even after trancing I feel like I don't know him at all. I know he's big and strong, because when he entered my body, that's how I felt, but I need Gegu's help to describe him more accurately.

James is tall, solid and all muscle. He likes to fight and is not comfortable speaking, but he has a smoldering quality that women are attracted to. His face isn't like his brother's or his mother's; it is more like Joseph's—sculptured and square, with dark, brooding eyes. His hair is thick and black and cascades over a tense brow.

The next time we trance, on November 13, 2000, James is more relaxed, and we work well together. I feel I have gained his trust because he is more animated and moves my hands as he speaks.

James

"My first memory of Jesus was when I was about two years old. I was lying in my crib on a soft goatskin blanket—the very same blanket Jesus had used—looking at the world, when suddenly Jesus popped his head over the side. He smiled and looked at me with those incredible blue eyes.

"When I was learning to walk, Jesus and Ruth would take a hand each and lead me around the house. It was always a busy household, and it was normal for the older children to take active roles in the raising of the youngsters.

"It was common to start doing chores between the ages of four and five, and it was my job to sweep the courtyard and remove the manure from the stables. When Jesus was not with Ruth and Mary, he would willingly help. On this particular day, he helped me, then took me for a walk down to the beach. Jesus was seven, and I enjoyed my time with him. It was only later, after our father had unsettled me, I began to tease him.

"When we neared the beach, a few fishing boats were unloading their catch. It was always a busy, social place. As the fishermen were carrying their baskets of fish to shore, one of the smaller fish would occasionally slip out. Jesus and I, weaving amongst everyone, picked them up. Some of these fish were feeble, and I would hand them to Jesus, who would blow on them and put them back into the sea.

"This became a game for us. I would find the fish, Jesus would put them back into the sea, and the fish would swim away. Now, as an adult looking back, I realize some of those fish were dead, but that was no problem for my big brother: he'd hold them, smile at me, and set them free.

"When I was six, I started to travel with Joseph; sometimes with Jude, and sometimes not, if he was fishing with Zebedee. On these journeys it was my job to tend to the donkey. Whenever we stopped for water, I'd fill a goatskin bucket for the donkey and tend to its needs. I was responsible for tying it up at night, collecting wood or manure for the fire and unfurling the sleeping blankets.

"Joseph had a favorite tent made of three or four hides sewn together. It had a particular smell, musky and smoky, and, although I never took to smoking, I always enjoyed the aroma. Two corners of the hide were held down with rocks, while the other two were supported with short poles. If we had to sleep out, this was enough to protect us from wind and moisture.

"On one of these journeys, we went to Bethsaida so my father could preach. We stayed in the home of Abe and Jessica, who had three daughters. They fed us a hearty meal, after which we retired to the stable to sleep. We lived so closely with animals that we didn't find their habits or odors offensive at all.

"I woke in the night, and at first I thought I was at home, until I saw Jessica straddling my father. I stared at her out of curiosity and I remember being aroused, or as close as you can be when you are seven. My prying eyes must have alerted Jessica, because she turned to me in fright, hastily dismounted my father and ran towards her lodgings, her white buttocks wobbling in the moonlight.

"I can laugh at this memory now, but at the time, I was only seven and a half, and it flustered me. I turned to my father who, without any trace of shame or embarrassment, grinned and told me to go back to sleep.

"My father and I spoke of this incident—an event that was to become common—the next day. Those secrets became our bond, but what hurt me was the shame I carried for him when I saw my mother and siblings. I wished my big brother could have helped with this burden, for it was too much responsibility for a child to carry.

"I was away with our father when Jesus left for Assyria with Joseph of Arimathea. I was fourteen, and this time we had journeyed to a small village outside of Jerusalem. We lodged with Rithyn and Athena this night. Rithyn was a large, weathered man, while Athena was a good twenty years his junior. They had no children. We slept in the loft this night, away from the main dwelling.

"During our evening meal, the men consumed the wine Athena served them, and Rithyn, who was not good with his drink, was soon out cold. Later that night, I was already in the loft when my father led Athena over. He was drunk and unstable on his feet, and I watched them disrobe and sink to the floor. Athena was soon doing things with her mouth that I had never before imagined.

"Tonight would be different from our other trips away, for this time I would not just be a voyeur, but would become an active participant. My father and I took turns. He seduced her with his charm, while I excited her with my youth. Athena was not my first, for I had overcome one of the local girls down by the beach, but I never imagined a woman could be so willing.

"We did unthinkable things to another man's wife while he lay slumbering over the way. My father eventually tired and drifted off to sleep, but Athena and I continued on until dawn. I was young and strong, but I could not overcome this Athena. She took me in her mouth and in her other place, and I tasted her most intimate parts while she panted and whispered the foulest words.

"It was not the sex that shamed me, but the weight of the secret I had to hide from my mother, my sisters, and my beautiful big brother. The shame I carried was my father's; he had imprisoned me with his guilt. The resentment I felt for Jesus grew only from my need of him, for I loved him dearly.

"When Jesus was twenty-three, he asked me to follow him as a disciple. At first, I accepted, and we did many great things together. He gave me healing skills and opened my heart, but I deserted him, and walked away with my Sarah. I walked away from his faith.

"I thank you. We are friends, and now, I will find my brother Jude for you."

James's memory of his father with Jessica is painful and confusing for him. This event shaped his life, even more than choosing to be a disciple. James's loyalty to his father's betrayal strained his relationships with his immediate family.

It is a brave thing for a man to do, sharing his darkest secrets with another man, and I am honored he has called me friend.

JUDE

It is November 15, 2000, and over the last few days Jude has been keeping me company while I work; chatting to me while watching me cut and glue pipes together. I'm sure, if he was able, he'd pick up a shovel and help. When we drive from one job site to the next, he sits in the passenger seat with his arm resting on the windowsill as if he's done it all before.

Smiling and relaxed, he watches as I turn on the radio. He's tapping his foot in time with the beat. When we drive past a couple of girls, I catch him looking, and then he turns to me and smiles and raises his eyebrows. It surprises me how visible Jude is, how *physical* he is, both here and at home.

Generally, when spirits wish to speak to me, I see them in *their* environment. Jesus and his family usually appear in the countryside around Nazareth, or on the beaches of Galilee, and when they speak to me, I witness the episodes in their lives they are sharing. When I am typing, however, spirit stands beside me in the flesh.

After arriving home, we go downstairs to trance, and I have a meditation before we begin. I visit the valley of the David rescues to see if any children are there, and Jude asks to come, so we walk the familiar path together. A group of children are sitting together playing, so I sit amongst them and a book materializes in my hands. Jude settles himself and pulls two children into his lap. When I start to read, Jude, beaming from ear to ear, plaits daisies into a young girl's hair.

Looking up from my reading, I see waves of rainbow colored light and golden rays reaching into the valley. Celeste steps from the light, waves, and beckons us. Turning to Jude I say, "It's time to go," and together we walk towards Celeste. Jude is giving a young boy a shoulder ride and holding the hand of another.

We amble up the rise, and in the pathway of light, we can see the smiling faces of loved ones who have already passed. They are waiting for the children. Celeste smiles and kisses me, which she always does, when I pass a baby to her. If you can remember the breathless excitement of your first kiss, that's what Celeste's kisses feel like; she kisses right into where the butterflies hide. I look at Jude and think his cheeks must be hurting he is smiling so much. After I introduce him to Celeste, she embraces him, and I think he blushes.

Jude and I return home to trance, and initially, he has difficulty recalling memories of his brother. With Jude in me, I know he is casual and relaxed and doesn't put any importance on everyday events. I know Jude is a happy boy who lets everything pass him by. He loves his big brother because he makes him smile, and that is all he seems to care about.

Jude

"I'm trying to think of something to tell you, but I must confess I'm struggling. I know I teased Jesus unnecessarily when I was younger, but I spent more time with James and I followed his lead.

"I do remember being sick one time with the coughing sickness. Mother Mary and Miriam bathed me in warm water to settle me and made me drink something that smelled foul. I think I was about six, so Jesus would have been ten. I remember him leaning against the doorway, watching our mother fuss and smiling at me.

"When she let me be, he wandered towards me and smiled one of his infectious smiles, and just like that, the cough was gone; with just one of his smiles, my cough had disappeared. He hugged me and gave me a bit of a shove then walked over to the fire and dished up some soup. We sat and ate lunch together.

"When Mother Mary returned, I told her, "Look, Mother. I'm well—the cough's gone." All I wanted to do was to go outside and play. Ha, I'm laughing at this now, but at the time I thought nothing of it. I was only six and I was just happy to stop coughing.

"Another time, I think I was younger, I was collecting eggs when I was stung on the hand by one of the black scorpions common to our region. To my recollection, Jesus had been at the market with Ruth and Mary Magdalene. After being bitten, and feeling unwell, I walked back to the house and sat in the shade. When I looked up I saw my brother running towards me.

"He clambered over the courtyard wall and hurried over to me. He looked at me and said, "It's okay, Jude, I know what's happened, and I can help you." Then he held my hand and said the strangest thing: "Your angel cried out to me." I had no idea what he was talking about.

"He put some spit on the bite and rubbed it in. Soon the pain I had been feeling was gone. He helped me to my feet and roughed me up a bit, but when Ruth and Mary Magdalene arrived home, he was hugging me. They were flustered and worried because Jesus had run from them, but Jesus merely grinned and said that everything was fine.

"He spent the rest of the morning with me and we cleaned the yard and stable, then we pestered Grandmother Anna until she gave us some fresh bread. I loved being in the kitchen with her. She would pretend to be too busy to notice me, but I knew that if I persisted, she would give me something to eat. I loved her. I think Jesus was her favorite, but it never bothered me; I shared myself with everyone.

"I remember going to work with my father Joseph. I was young the first time, but I never questioned why Jesus didn't come. My father's womanizing didn't affect me as much as it did James, and I was shocked to hear him tell you his story. I had noticed his spirit had hardened over the years, but he was a good man, and I love him still.

"When I was twelve, Jesus was sixteen, and he took me with him to Capernaum. We left early in the morning, and rather than take the road, we walked along the shore. We stopped for a swim and dried ourselves in the sun. Afterwards we ate bread for lunch and looked at the sea.

"'Can you see them? Can you see them coming?' he asked me.

"I looked at him and looked out to sea again, but I could see nothing. I nudged him in the ribs. "You're jesting me."

"'No, Jude. They're coming, and they're coming for me,"

"'Okay, who's coming?' I said, playing along with him.

"'The dark one; the dark one is beside us. He wants my soul, and he wants my flesh, but it is not time."

"Now I was getting worried, because he was so serious, and I knew he was truthful. Reaching for his hand, I tried to reassure him. "It's okay, big brother. I will look after you. I will be there with you."

"'You will be one of many. One day you will watch me die, and you will see our people turn away from the good that we believe in."

"Looking across at him, I saw tears running down his cheeks, and, as I reached out to catch a tear, I saw them. I saw the angels—not the dark ones he was speaking of, but beautiful angels. If I had not held his tear I would have been afraid. It was at this moment that I knew, one day I would follow him to his death. This saddened me, and I had nothing more to say.

"I leaned against him and we looked out to sea together, but we were seeing different things. I believed then that I knew why he cried when he slept, and why at times he could not find peace. I knew why he sought comfort with the women, and why he was uncomfortable around my cheating father. I never teased him after that day, and I stopped my bullying. I became a man that day.

"We continued our journey to Capernaum, and eventually Itharus welcomed us into his home. He was a jolly man and greeted us with hugs and laughter. Itharus was the roundest, chubbiest man I had ever seen, and his cheeks were so large that you could barely see his eyes, while his mouth seemed too small for his face.

"We ate and laughed together, and when I tired, I lay down next to the fire. The warmth was seductive, and I soon fell asleep listening to Itharus and Jesus talking. I didn't know what they were talking about, but I loved the sound of my brother's voice—it soothed me to sleep.

"Waking in the middle of the night, I found my brother sleeping next to me, but he was also standing in the doorway. He looked down at me, smiled and put his finger to his lips. "Go to sleep, I have work to do," and then he was gone—well, one of him was gone—and I drifted back to sleep. When I woke in the morning, Jesus had already risen and was talking quietly to Itharus, so I imagined I had merely been dreaming.

"When we walked home, we didn't want to waste any time so we took the road. We were happy and our step was light. Suddenly, Jesus stopped, turned to me and asked, "Jude, what's your angel's name?" It wasn't the question that surprised me, but that I was able to answer him. Looking at him I answered, "Aisshlon." He started to laugh and ran on ahead of me. I soon caught him and laughed with him. He was so beautiful.."

Jude pauses, and Gegu drapes his arm around both of us. My body sighs and releases Jude's loss.

"You could say I have led a sheltered life with the family. Maybe it was simply that I didn't let things affect me, like those things that hurt James and Rachael.

"Did I have a favorite in the family?"

Jude gives a long sigh.

"Yes, I had a favorite. Louise was my favorite. She was younger than me, and I loved her. When I grew into a man, I loved her even more. You know, I never married because my love for Louise was so strong. I will speak about her next time.

"There are many more who wish to speak to you. You are a man I could drink with. I'll be back."

I like Jude, and out of all the men, he is the one I have felt most comfortable with. With Gegu's help, I learned he was a good friend of Judas, who I know was not popular with many of the other disciples. I'd stand back and keep to myself and say little unless spoken to. I was the only disciple who was an outsider. I'd approached Jesus and asked to be a follower. The others were family, friends and locals. Jude always included me in every discussion; he valued my opinion, and, many times, he stood up for me and encouraged my healing gift. He never let me be too serious, and it was thanks to him that I was able to find the confidence to support Jesus.

Like a hologram projected from my mind I can see the two of us playing some game with pebbles and small tablets. We are drinking wine and watching ladies walk by.

A conversation we had comes back to me; as I turn away from Jude, he pulls me into the shade and embraces me fiercely. When he releases me his hands remain on my shoulders and he is looking into my eyes. His brow is furrowed and his eyes plead with me.

"You must not do this thing. You must not ask it of him."

This is in reference to my desire to see a display of Jesus' power. This is what compelled me to betray him. I wished for Jesus to confront his enemies, and I did not understand that true power is the power of love and forgiveness.

"Will you turn from me?"

"I must; he is my brother."

"What shall I do?"

"What he knows you will."

With this, I walk away from Jude. I look back once, but he is already gone. I feel indecisive and afraid. Jude returns to his family, and I betray Jesus.

A slave trader, who had contacts with the palace staff of Herod Antipas, handled the transaction for the betrayal. The information I traded was passed to a high priest who, in order to gain favor with Herod Antipas and seal his position in the upper council of the Sanhedrin, ordered Jesus' arrest. Jesus was arrested by Herod's troops and condemned to death by the Sanhedrin.

Pontius Pilate was afraid for his and his family's lives. If he could not control the rising unrest in Judea, Rome would punish him and his family. Herod and his troops were little more than paid mercenaries for Rome, and it was Herod and the Sanhedrin who condemned Jesus. Pilate was easily manipulated because of the rising tensions at the time.

The price of the betrayal was not thirty pieces of silver, as was widely believed. I negotiated a side deal for more than one hundred pieces of silver to finance Jesus' ministry, believing that after Jesus had been captured he would break his bonds and overwhelm the Sanhedrin council, silence them, seal their lips with a gesture and prove he was the Son of God.

Seal their lips with a gesture. I look over my shoulder for Wes Craven because he must be nearby directing a cast without lips. I typed this passage so quickly the words didn't register. I'll change my sandals for Nikes and Mount Sinai for Uluru.

I gambled that Jesus would be taken before the council unharmed. I was mistaken. He was beaten and tortured and imprisoned in a dungeon with sodomites, murderers and thieves, and denied food and water. Battered, dehydrated and weak, he was unable to speak and needed to be supported to stand. He didn't carry the cross to the execution site; he was dragged and publicly humiliated.

Jesus had challenged the priests of his time. He had undermined the power of their temples and their political and social positions in the community. Once they had captured Jesus, therefore, they wanted him silenced.

I was naïve. The go-between never had the authority to broker a deal with me, and both he and the high priest were only interested in advancing their own positions for financial and political gain.

Jesus was the people's prophet. He had no desire to stand before temple priests who elevated themselves with false titles and supported a military regime. He has described himself as a socialist, and empowered communities to pool their resources: feed the hungry, shelter the homeless, distribute wealth and find God in life.

He spoke to people where they gathered: in their homes, their markets, their fields, and fishing grounds. He placed his hands on the sick, and, to show their gratitude, families, villages, merchants, and nomads gave him food and lodgings. This provided him with the opportunity to speak, and people listened.

Some of the disciples grew restless. They tired of the road, the secrecy, the danger and argued that Jesus should confront the priests and politicians. Jesus remained silent. Judas stood apart, isolated, and Jesus' eyes would find mine. A silent message passes between us:

"What will you do?"

All the disciples and many of Jesus' followers had seen Jesus move through a crowd, and the crowd part. There was always space around him. What forces kept the excited crowds at bay?

From Jesus, "What will you do?"

"In time they will find us."

"Yes. There will be bloodshed."

Jesus never raised a hand. He had repeatedly told me his hands were for healing and not for striking our enemies. Jesus did not want to prove he was the Son of God; he wanted his followers to know that they were God's people.

God cannot be found in churches or places of worship; he is inside us. Judas missed that lesson, and I haven't understood until now. The only beast we need to battle resides within us. It is fear.

If Jesus and his followers had toppled the priests and militant leaders, greedy politicians would have governed the people. Smiling dictators would have replaced snarling tyrants, and the people would remain disadvantaged and poor.

Jesus kept this insight hidden from the arguing disciples. History has proved him to be correct. He did not sacrifice himself for our sins. He was murdered. Our sins sacrificed him.

Jesus united communities by being present. He didn't rule from a palace. He replaced fear with hope and servitude with service. His mission was to create change with compassion: to share wealth, harvest, trade, and knowledge.

Jesus didn't sacrifice himself for humanity. Tyrants dragged him to his death, and many of his followers became silent witnesses. Others fled and, over time, his teachings were used to create one of the things he had tried to overthrow—a church.

Judas' pain at being responsible for his brother's death drove him to hang himself. I hung myself because I couldn't face the disciples, Mary Magdalene, and the son Jesus had fathered.

Jude is here again, hugging me as I type. "You did what you had to. I liked Judas, but I like Simon more." His brother has taught him well. He both strengthens and forgives me.

BETH

Beth arrived with Jude on November 15, 2000, and has been in my ear all day; persistent and willing to talk. I can't help warming to this tough old woman. She is quick to call a spade a spade and is partial to throwing the odd profanity in for effect, but I'm pleased she didn't pick the swear words I use.

Beth scoffed at the notion that I needed to trance. "Just get on the computer and type, young man."

Beth controlled me and didn't let me rest. By the time we finished, my fingers were sore. Having never typed before I started this project, it was quite a feat for me to keep up with Beth. "Bollocks," she said. "This is what the funny man has been training you for."

"Thank you, Beth."

Beth

"Hello, young man. I have been waiting patiently for you to let me speak. I have noticed the young ones have not chosen to speak for me, which is just as well. I never needed anyone to speak for me in the past, and I'm not about to start now!

"Now, this is none of your business, young man, and don't think I will share my bedroom secrets with you like those young ones who came before me, but I found myself a man: a strong, hard man, a straight talker, the weathered and lean Aramiss, the fisherman who adopted Lucha like a son. We shared his stone abode down on the beach, away from the gossiping folk of Nazareth, and when Lucha came, I fussed over him like a son.

"My friendship with Anna remained strong, and I visited often. There was hardly a day when we did not see each other, except when her Joachim was home; the lustful bugger.

"I'd often see Jesus with his sister, Ruth, and Mary Magdalene. They were always polite and helped carry my goods. Ruth and Mary Magdalene were inseparable and, sure enough, little Jesus was never far away. He spent a lot of time with the girls, and why not, with a father like that.

"I saw Rachael bathing Jesus after his beating. The man was a pig. Jesus was always so gentle and did not need to be beaten like that. He was often crying. I found him many times on his own, sniffling like a baby, but I could never be hard on him—you only had to look at him to see how soft he was. Of course I knew something about him, something I only ever shared with my brother.

"One day, when he must have been ten or eleven, I noticed him walking along the beach. He came up to me while I was collecting greens for my medicines. He was burdened with a sad face, so we found a place to sit and looked out to sea.

"I sat him between my legs, and he leaned back into my breasts. Now only my Aramiss was allowed to do that, but he filled me, and I knew it was him—the one I had seen, but had only suspected until now. He told me about his restless nights, the voices, the angels, and I already knew about his meeting with Simeon and the afternoon he had spent with my brother.

"He told me of his healing gift, and how many times he had surprised his family and friends. Many knew he was different, and there was talk of him being deranged. Folk and their gossip; how they sicken me. I listened to the boy, and then he said quietly, "Grandmother Beth, I have to save our people, and I am so afraid." Then he cried. I rocked him like a baby and knew I had to tell him.

"You see, I'm like you: I talk to angels. If anyone had known, I'd have been stoned for being a witch. The men would have used this as an excuse for raping me, and when they were done, they would have bled me like a pig. Our age was violent and unforgiving. So many times we were shown God, and so many times we turned from Him. Moses wasted his time on us. We did not deserve his passion.

"When I was in my teens, I foresaw a birth under the stars. When this fated child walked amongst his people, the land was overcome with an army. The army was an all-consuming fire of hate and falsehood, and as this child grew into a man, I saw no cross, but I did see him crying tears of blood. I told Jesus this man was Him; you are the Messiah that is spoken of, and you must prepare yourself; my gift has remained hidden; yours will not.

"He listened, and we stayed together until sunset. When I next saw him, he was a child again, scrapping with his brothers. His childhood was as changeable as the seas of my Aramiss, so it is no wonder he was so easily brought to tears.

"After being caught in a downpour, I came down with a chest sickness. Having always been a stubborn old thing, I'd take no help from Anna, nor would I let my Aramiss tend to me himself. On the way home late one evening, having gone down to the shore hoping to catch Aramiss bringing his fishing boat in, I fell. I was in such poor shape that I was unable to get to my feet.

"Jesus appeared, smiled down at me, scolded me gently and lifted me to my feet. He was only fourteen, but the cheeky bugger kissed me. When his lips found my cheek, incredible warmth coursed through me. His face was glowing, and he laughed and asked if I'd like to be accompanied home. We walked home holding hands. I simply can't believe it—we walked home holding hands.

"Joseph died when Jesus was away on the first of his many trips. Good riddance, I said. I still don't know how Mary stood by him. I knew what the bastard had done to Rachael, and I think Anna may have suspected, too.

Anna and I were good friends, but there were many things we did not speak on. She was the head of her family, and her business was her business.

"When she passed, I was twelve years her senior, and now my best friend was gone. My Aramiss had passed three years earlier, and I had lived with her ever since, for our fishing cottage was too lonely without my bowlegged man. I still miss him. Let us leave this story for Anna. God bless."

Tonight, I'm proofreading Beth's story and thinking about Jesus. I haven't felt him for a few days, and I'm wondering if he is here. Suddenly, my shoulders and the back of my neck start to tingle, and he says, "Hello." I see him walking towards me through my army of man-beasts, who part like the Red Sea and come to attention. I haven't used them for a while, but I can feel their energy swirling around me. David is near, for I have seen him resting beside me.

Jesus speaks to me.

"They are restless."

"Yes, it is David who stirs them."

"No, it is you, Simon. They look to you to lead them to an ancient battleground where many great healers and warriors were overrun by darkness and lost their lives to conquering hordes."

"Why are you speaking to me about this when we are writing on your life?"

"This is only one of the lives I have led. A part of my spirit remains on that bloody field. My Father asks that you release the many spirits trapped by the darkness. Death is painless, yet many spirits are trapped by the fear that subdued their flesh.

"David can free those spirits so they may return to the cradle of my Father. The spirits of the ancient, nomadic healers who were slain on that field will be reborn as healers in your world, and the knowledge they possess will be used to move the Earth to a higher energy."

"Why do you share this with the Beth story?"

"A part of her spirit also remains on that field. She was not led to my birth by chance, and I was led to her illness by the same guiding force. She was more than the midwife at my birth; she was the energy needed to ignite the light within me. Each one of the members of my family served a higher purpose.

"Emotion is what activates the God within. We are flesh, and emotion is the life force that ignites our flame. What we consider a burden is actually our greatest gift. The challenge of overcoming our negative emotions strengthens our spirit.

"Grandmothers Beth and Anna, together with Mother Mary, eased me into this world so I could show all of you the possibilities trapped within. You struggle to hear me, and you struggle to see me, but emotion is about feeling, and when you feel me, you become me. I leaned against Beth's breasts to feel her heartbeat, and then I could heal her. If you cannot feel, you cannot connect with God. All the people in my life had the right emotions so that I could become more than Jesus.

"Can you not see beyond your lives? Can you not feel your neighbor's anguish, the anguish of being a neighbor? He does not wish to be separate from you; he is different, that is all. The reality is that he is the same as you, because without his energy you would not exist. Your energy is made stronger not by overpowering the energy of others, but by accepting that this new feeling is just an old feeling long forgotten."

HANNAH

It is November 17, 2000 and Hannah, the daughter of Zebedee and Miriam, has been talking to me for two days. She has brown, shoulder-length hair and brown eyes with seductive long lashes. Her petite frame supports full hips and generous breasts and her golden skin is sprinkled with freckles. Kiss-me lips outline her I-love-the-world smile.

She's leaning forward to watch me type, and her breast is brushing against my shoulder. I can feel the warmth radiating off her body, and her body odor takes my breath away. I feel flustered and she hugs me from behind, which doesn't help. She sits beside me on an imaginary seat, leaving one hand resting on my shoulder. I can feel her smiling at me while waiting for me to continue.

Everyone knows someone like Hannah. If she walked into a room, all the men would turn to stare, and the women would instinctively move closer to their husbands.

Hannah's story is important, because she was unaffected by Jesus' gift.

Hannah has confessed to being a nymphomaniac, but only once did her sexual excesses cause her any shame. For the rest of her life, she accepted who she was and did not care what other people thought about her.

Hannah is a confident, happy person with an unending supply of love for her family. She is a hard worker and respectful of both her family and herself. She was a pleasure to work with. Her story is important, because she was the only one who saw Jesus as just another man she could unsettle with her sexual appetite, and Jesus was happy about that because at times, that is all he wished to be.

Hannah

"I loved my family, but I loved my father Zebedee the most. He was big and strong, yet always gentle and loving with me. When I was a baby, I'd crawl into his arms and go off to sleep. He always had time for me, and I loved the way he smelled and the feel of his rough hands.

"At the time of my birth I developed a chest infection and struggled physically for many years. When my Father fished overnight, I slept with my mother and brothers, all snuggled up together.

"Luke first went fishing with Zebedee when he was four. They were inseparable, and it was only when the seas were rough that he was not allowed to go. Luke was quick to learn and would literally fall asleep on his feet, whereupon Zebedee would lay him on a goatskin and continue fishing.

"Michael didn't start fishing seriously until he was eight. He didn't have the passion for it like Luke did. Zebedee had only one fishing dhow at this stage, and his older brother Matthew, who was a quiet man and good with the boys, crewed with him. Mathew died when I was six. He was a lot older than my father and passed in his sleep. Even though he had not lived with us, we all missed him.

"The boys crewed with Zebedee then, until Luke, at only eleven years of age, was entrusted with his own boat. Zebedee asked old Aramiss to crew with Luke. Without undermining his youthful exuberance, Aramiss taught Luke all he knew.

"I remember the day Jesus arrived home, because I had missed Mother Mary and was pleased she was home. I enjoyed being around her and my mother and, despite being sickly, they always included me in everything. They never treated me like a sick child, and I am thankful for the confidence they instilled in me.

"Though we didn't spend much time together when I was growing up, I had also missed Grandma Anna. She was always busy with everyone else, and because I was on my mother's hip for so many years, we never bonded. I liked her baking, and if I were in the right place at the right time, she'd always give me cooked treats and kisses.

"I'm unable to share any stories of Jesus' miracles because I think they just went over my head. It seems my head was always in the clouds.

"I remember James and John being born. Because I was older, I got to show them the ropes. I enjoyed having playmates. Swimming together at the beach was a highlight for us all.

"One of my chores was to unload fish with my brothers, and as I got older, I'd help with the drying and smoking of those fish that were not sold fresh. Salt was used in the curing process, and when I was a teenager I always had sore hands, but I preferred to work outdoors rather than with needle and thread with my mother.

"When Rachael came to live with us I was three. I remember Mother Mary crying all the time and being comforted by my mother. Rachael fit in well. We never fought and were never jealous of each other, and Zebedee loved us both.

"He was a giant of a man, yet so compassionate, and I frequently saw him comforting Mother Mary, which warmed my heart. He had a booming, gruff voice that made those who didn't know him nervous, but to his family, he was a gentle giant.

"Rachael was a bit of a tomboy, and for many years was always stronger than me. She wasn't a bully, just bossy. She had a good sense of humor and was always daring. By the time I was ten; I started to match her. I had finally filled out and was over my chest infections, but I still didn't look three years older than her.

"She was a robust, wild-haired dynamo, and there wasn't much that ever bothered her. She did become a little quiet between the ages of twelve and thirteen, but I assumed it was because she always bled heavily and was embarrassed, so I was sorry to hear her tell her story.

"I must say, I never warmed to Joseph. By the time I was twelve, I was aware of his womanizing. Mother Mary was courageous to put up with it. Everyone knew everyone in Nazareth, and it was hard to keep a secret, but the gossip and innuendo didn't seem to affect Mary.

"Paul and Mathew had been welcome additions to our family. Our mother was always happiest when she was breastfeeding; I'm sure she had enough milk for the whole family. When Mathew was born, I was eight, and a year later, James and John were fishing regularly.

"Our father was content when he had boys to teach, and he had many small boats by this stage. Luke was big and loved the sea like Zebedee, while Michael was happy to follow directions. Zebedee had no favorites; He loved all his children equally: in public with vigor and authority, and at home with tenderness and warmth.

"We are a clean people who wash our hands and feet regularly, and when we were younger, we bathed by swimming in the sea. Some of the older men continued this practice, but the women bathed by sponging their bodies with warm water and then applying scented lotions.

"Our bathing area was in the stable, screened with hides and woven blankets, and the wastewater was used on our gardens. Our toilet waste was also used on our gardens, this unpleasant chore being shared.

"One day, while I was bathing, I caught Jesus watching me. He was nine, and I was fifteen. He had been collecting eggs and saw me when he bent to pick one up. I do not know how long he had been there when I realized he was watching me, and I shouldn't have teased him, but I moved so he could see my labia, and I washed myself more than I needed to. From his crouched position, it was clear I had excited him, because I could see his erection. When he realized I was looking at him, he ran off in embarrassment and could not look at me for days afterwards.

"In my teens, I was full of desire, and I'd go to the beach at every opportunity and watch the older boys bathe. I'd stay hidden and touch myself, and it was one of the bathing boys to whom I gave my virginity. I was thirteen, and it hurt a little, but it was over too quickly and left me wanting more. We did it many more times later. Soon there wasn't anything sexually I wouldn't do. Boys and men were always willing, and I was out of control, insatiable.

"Jesus and I often travelled together to Capernaum for his lessons with Itharus, and it was there that I met Orpheus. He was a shy, handsome twenty-year-old, whom I eventually married at the age of twenty-three. We moved to Cairo, and had two lovely children, and while I was not faithful, I was discreet, and we lived happily ever after.

"I did not witness Jesus' death, nor did I return home at that time. It was later I returned with my children to visit their beautiful grandparents and our extended family.

"I had a wonderful upbringing, and I love my family dearly. I have just one more tale for you, so that you realize Jesus was a boy who grew into a man, easily tempted by my flesh, just as the other boys were.

"It was on the way home from one of our visits to Capernaum. I was nineteen, and Jesus was thirteen. We had stopped to rest in the shade, and while we were talking, I sat brazenly so he was able to see up my shift, fidgeting casually so he had a better view. He was embarrassed and flushed, but he could not look away.

"He was always so shy and emotional, and I knew he was gifted, someone special, but I had not been affected by the amazing things that happened around him. To me, he was Jesus, the boy I teased while bathing, and he was part of my family: I loved him.

"Knowing that he wanted to touch me, I let him. I had to guide his hand so that he touched me properly, and then I helped him. As I held him, he shuddered. We both cried, which was an unusual reaction for me.

Later, I was able to be faithful to my Orpheus for a short time, so perhaps Jesus had affected me after all."

Hannah kisses me politely on the cheek when I have finished typing. Her body odor is enchanting, and I enjoy her lingering scent. It has been Hannah's honesty I have felt the most while working with her.

A sexual energy surrounds her, but since I've become accustomed to it, I realize how intelligent she is. She's confident, and I've enjoyed her informal style of speech.

When Hannah was talking about curing fish, I saw fishermen carrying baskets of fish to the curing sheds. The fish had already been sorted into baskets of sardines, biny and musht, and were carried ashore by nearly-naked fisherman who looked like they were wearing large, loose nappies. All the men were bearded and tanned from the sun, and would look good on the cover of *Sports Illustrated*, or in a fireman's uniform.

They used large ovens to smoke and dry the biny and musht. After scaling and gutting the fish, a job performed mostly by slave labor, the flesh of the fish was immersed in brine. The larger fish had salt rubbed into their flesh and were skewered on wooden poles and hung in rows above smoldering embers.

Flax, watercress, and another unidentified plant were laid above the coals on iron rods and used to smoke the fish. The ovens were constructed out of slabs of stone, so that the coals burned slowly, and the airflow was controlled so the flax and watercress did not ignite and burn too quickly, while hinged wooden shutters, which were immersed in water after each curing, contained the heat and smoke.

This process took four hours, and then the fish were lightly salted once again and packed in baskets for export. The ovens were used communally, but the fisherman's family or hired labor did the final packing.

Sometimes these ovens operated night and day, while a tax collector oversaw the process and recorded each fisherman's catch. The community and the fishermen were taxed according to the sale price negotiated with the exporter, but because of the high taxes, it was difficult to earn an adequate income. To avoid taxation fish were often sold wet, either from the boats or on the sea.

Hannah's story unsettles Narelle. She is disturbed by the sexual content and believes spirit will not divulge anything sexually, but I have no preconceptions about how spirits communicate, or what they will talk about.

Narelle became distant after reading it, but didn't immediately voice her discord. The irony is that when I trance with Narelle present, she sees at least part of what I am narrating and experiences all of the emotions.

I don't know how to ease her uncertainty. In between working with Jesus and his family I had tranced Narelle's son. The style of my voice, adopted mannerisms, and the conversation her son had with her convinced her, "you're the best trance medium I've ever seen." She's torn between knowing she was speaking to her son, and her Catholic education.

I sympathize with her dilemma, but I cannot ignore Jesus and his family. The speed at which they're visiting has not given me time to think, and I am constantly surprised by what I am hearing.

SARAH, WIFE OF JAMES FROM THE HOME OF JOSEPH

Sarah is James' wife. She first spoke to me while I was showering on January 3, 2001. She is shy, and blushes easily. The love she feels for James and their children is overwhelming. She has a homely figure, wavy, mousey-blonde hair, which surprises me, and big, round blue eyes.

I keep expecting everyone to have Middle Eastern characteristics: dark hair, dark eyes, and a tanned complexion. Sarah's eyes look wet, as if she's been crying, and the blue keeps changing—she has spirit eyes, not human eyes.

She keeps looking down and looks away when I soap and rinse myself. I've noticed because she is the first and only spirit to react this way. She says she will not be as forward as the other girls and hopes I understand. I find her quite endearing and tease her gently, at which she blushes and chuckles softly. I've yet to have my back washed by a visiting ghost, but I remain hopeful.

Sarah is standing beside me as I type her trance. She is smiling and teasing me when I struggle with my typing. I ask her if she knew Judas.

"Yes. He spoke little and stood apart from the others. He had sad eyes, and he always seemed uncomfortable around me. I think that was because he was respectful of James."

Sarah

"My father's name was Ibrahim, and he was a fisherman who lived in Nazareth. I was named after my mother, who died in a tragic accident when I was two years old. She was helping my father repair his fishing boat when the log supporting it slipped, and the falling boat crushed her. My father's love for her was pure: he never remarried or lay with another woman. He taught me how to love, and he taught me about faith.

"I was six years younger than James, and we married when I was nineteen. I had loved him from the time I had first met him, at the age of twelve. What a fine man he was. People respected him, for he was strong-willed and stood up for his family. Everyone in Nazareth knew Joseph's character, but they would not say a bad word against him in front of James.

"James's shame troubled him heavily, and he shared it with me. I forgave him as soon as he spoke but, alas, he could never forgive himself. The burden of his father's secrets haunted him always.

"I knew Jesus was a special man. I knew his faith was strong, and I had heard tell of his healing gift. His eyes affected me, filling me with peace, and I was helpless in the face of the love he had for his brothers.

"James travelled often with Jesus, but spoke little of the deeds he performed with his brother. I am not sure what troubled him so, but he often returned tired and quiet. I think he felt lost in his brother's faith, and was unsure of his own, but did not wish to fail his older brother. In time, he came to fear for his brother's safety.

"Our first child was born when I was twenty-four. It was at this time that James pulled away from his brother, for he was afraid for his son and me. It was not common for men to be present for a birth in those times, but both James and Jesus attended me and held my hands, and I felt no pain at all. Jesus blessed my child then left James to tend to me. He laid beside me through the night, this beautiful, gentle father who tended to his son's needs. I loved him so much.

"His heart was broken when his brother was crucified. He tortured himself for not being there, and questioned his faith. When he returned to see his family, he did not take me with him, because he was fearful for my wellbeing, and for his son's safety.

"When he returned home, he often cried when he slept, and the soldiers defilement of his sisters filled him with anger that tore at his heart. In his prayers, he asked his brother to forgive him, and he asked God to forgive him. He tormented himself for having turned away from Jesus and his family.

"Not even the birth of our twin daughters, Rachael and Jessica, could ease James's troubled sleep. He would not release the burden of his brother's death until years later, when Jesus visited us again.

"The children were troubled with sickness, but James, who had not let go of his healing gift, was hesitant to use it because he thought he was not strong enough without his brother. Then, to our wonderment, his brother came.

"Jesus healed our children with his presence, and James cried in his brother's arms. Finally, with those tears, James was able to release his torment. When it was over, we lived the rest of our life together in love, peace and happiness.

"What a life we led together. James was a great carpenter. How I loved him. He was my one and only love, and the only man I ever lay with. What faith he showed me, which was something he had learned from his brother."

James is here too, now. I am sighing, and my throat is tight with emotion because they are happy I have written their stories.

James

"I watched my brother defy an empire to serve his people; and to what end? I walked away from him, and so did the people he had come to save.

They hung him on the cross, and the generations that followed kept him there. My heart is torn.

"Jesus showed me how to live by my heart, and not my fists or quick temper. It took his death and the birth of my children to realize the folly of my ways. Often, I fought with Roman soldiers to defend my brother, and Jesus, with his love, would heal and raise those soldiers to their feet. His forgiveness cannot be measured, and he judged no one nor raised his hands in anger. My brother lived his life by example, the most pure and love-filled example, only to be trampled upon by man.

"He brought God and faith to his people—he touched them—and they forgot, everyone forgot; and I include myself amongst them. As my brother, he was beautiful, and as a man, he was King—but he wished only to be a peasant King. He asked for no taxes; he asked not to be worshipped; he asked only for love—not for himself, but for all mankind.

"I have only loved my Sarah more, and the love I bear for my children, Jesus carried for all men. He was my brother, and I loved him."

My body is exhausted, and I have a metallic taste in my mouth. I feel like I'm lying on the floor, and James is looking down at me while he speaks. I'm surprised I'm still seated when he has finished.

James squeezes my shoulder, takes Sarah's hand, and together they walk away to sit with their children on the beach of Nazareth. Sarah turns and blows me a kiss, while James's son embraces him. I blink and when my eyes open, I'm staring at the wall.

JOHN THE BAPTIST

Narelle has talked about John the Baptist many times. She is curious whether or not he is related to Jesus and speculates about his death. In the Bible John the Baptist is beheaded after Salome, Herod Antipas' step-daughter, dances at Herod's birthday celebration and demands that John be executed. As she'd read an account of John's life in another channeled book, Narelle, wonders if this is correct.

John the Baptist arrived on January 17, 2001. I had been working with Jude and Hannah at the time, but they stepped aside for him. I have experienced this sign of respect only once before; and that was with the spirit of Moses.

When I sit down and play back the tape of our trance, John the Baptist is standing beside me. I have just come in from work, have made some toast and dished up some ice cream and canned peaches. I'm just about to eat when I hear him speak.

"Hello, Simon."

"Hi."

I almost call him Mr Baptist, because I have sensed how respectful Jude and Hannah were when he showed up. As if reading my mind, he says, "It's okay. You can call me John, young man." Which I'm grateful for because I'm nervous, and in my mind I'm playing with the French translation of his name; Jean Le Baptiste!

"Is that nice?" John's question confuses me, and it takes a second for me to realize he's talking about the ice cream and peaches.

"Ummm, yes."

"We never had anything like that in my day. What does it feel like in your mouth?"

I can feel him leaning forward, looking in the bowl. This is not what I had expected from him, especially after his forceful trance, and it was an unusual question. Not, what does it taste like?

"Well, it's soft and cold. You don't have to chew it, not even the peaches. It all just slides down together; the peaches are soft and sweet."

"Incredible. All these wonderful things." He's peering at the computer now. "And yet, we are still so primitive. Man can do so much good and yet still has not evolved; we are still so violent and destructive."

The energy from his statement silences my mind. I don't have a response. The silence isn't uncomfortable, and knowing he is genuinely interested in the ice cream has taken me by surprise. I know he would like to try some, which makes both of us smile, because obviously that is impossible.

John the Baptist

"When Jesus was born, I was forty years old. I had known of his coming since my early teens. I had been having visions of a young King and had been instructed by angels to bring this Messiah to the people.

"My father, Isaac, was a village priest. He raised me with the words of Abraham and Moses and schooled me in the history of our people. He had no time for a boy's visions, but my mother Martha was a loving woman who balanced my life with praise.

"I did not know where to find the Son of God, and it was my friend Itharus who led me to him. I had counsel with the child before his tenth birthday. We spoke of my faith and the cleansing ritual—the baptismal rite.

It was something I strongly believed in, but as Jesus grew, he knew it was only symbolic.

"While bathing in the clearest water, words were spoken to me: "Go forth and speak the truth. Go forth and share in the glory of the Father, and the coming of His Son." *And what son do you speak of,* I wondered. "The one born to a virgin bride," I was shown a young woman, childlike, with an aura of innocence. Her eyes were burdened with sadness, but no matter what overcame her in her lifetime, she would always retain a virginal innocence, but not the virginity of a maiden.

"To glory in this Messiah, to herald his arrival, I would be bathed in the clearest water. I had seen angels purifying children in the water, and now I was compelled to carry out this task myself.

"I spoke of these things to many of my friends, including many in the Sanhedrin, as my father was one of them, but I was a fool to trust these men. I was young and brash and thought these men had pure hearts, but they were puppets.

"The council of the Sanhedrin was more than seventy strong. Most of the villages in Judea and beyond were represented. Telling my visions to these men was my downfall. The high priests favored their positions and did not wish to be usurped by a Messiah.

"Herod was on the throne for Judea, and he sold his army to Rome. He was a false king and a mercenary for Rome. Many in the Sanhedrin were on his payroll.

"This is the shame of religious leaders: they spoil and twist reality for their own gain. They have the power of faith, but too many succumb to this power because, inside, they are weak and afraid. They believe what they see with their eyes, not what they feel with their hearts.

"The men of the Sanhedrin were corrupt, tainted by the sound of their own voices. They debated the life of Abraham and the words of David—the good king who raised an army and fought for his people—whose glory had been bestowed upon him by his people, not by the foreign rule that controlled Herod.

"Itharus and I schooled Jesus from his tenth year onwards. In his seventeenth year, he travelled to learn from other spiritual masters. We taught him how to read and write, how to use his faith and write from his heart. We taught him that no man has all the answers for faith; it is by blending the ideals of many and by living with faith that one will be led to God. It was his will to travel in order to learn, and we encouraged him in this, for he was a good student.

"I baptized Jesus when he was nineteen, along with James and John, in the prosperous farming community of Nabal. The river had changed course many times over the ages, depositing rich silt over a wide area, and the land was fertile. Jesus knew this was my way of bringing our people to God in order to spread His word.

"The people gathered to listen to His word, and Jesus kissed rich and poor alike. The clean and unclean came to feel his touch and to look into his eyes of love. He healed many. Those who could not walk he carried, and those who were pushed to the back he healed first: prostitutes with the weeping sickness, beggars with sores, and young children overlooked by hungry parents.

"These were the ones he healed and carried to the river, the ones who had accepted their life and asked for naught but the smile of the Messiah. He stirred the people of Nabal, but they quickly forgot, because upon his leave they fed and lusted on those healing banks.

"Jesus was twenty-three when I met my fate, which was not unexpected, for my angel had shown it to me many times. I was comforted by the thought I had served my faith. I had been true to myself: my mistake had been trusting men of false hope. I was not blind. I had served the Son of God, and I had shown him to my people. It was not my shame they proved unworthy.

"Herod was fat with ego and lusted after a young maiden, a whimsical creature who was attracted to his power. She could have had any handsome young man, but she chose to feast with this fat slob of a man.

"Herod had not always been fat, but Rome was keeping him in comfort at the expense of his sight, for he was blind to his people's needs. He was not blind to the charms of this fair maiden, however; this girl of fancy who asked for my head. Oh, what favors she bestowed on Herod, what deeds she did, and so my head she got.

"Having been jailed by the Romans for being a rebel who had caused unrest and turned the people against the Sanhedrin, I was easy to find. I had not turned the people against them, though; the Sanhedrin had become tax collectors, in league with the Romans, and there was fear in the land. Rome was a powerful empire, and her armies could crush us at any time, so people looked for favor.

"The Sanhedrin had become sheep following a false king. This was not supposed to be the way of the Sanhedrin. We were supposed to be messengers delivering faith to our people, travelling to neighboring communities and villages, sharing news and bringing our people together, but only a few were strong and faithful: Itharus, myself, and five others.

"History has been recorded by those with blood on their hands and fear in their hearts. It was my people who crucified Jesus, and it was too easy to lay blame on Rome. Jews had a hand in this, but now they proclaim the Holy Land, selling stories of His life.

"The words in the Bible were written by Jews, not Romans, and not by the Papal King. This is where the stories rest, distorted by time and greed. Faith has been stolen. It doesn't belong to one man; it belongs to all men. Where are the scrolls that tell the truth? Where are they? They will not be seen because then they would lose their power and their glory.

"The Catholic Church is full of powerful men, lustful and hungry for wealth, with all their pious rules. They say that man shall only sleep with woman. But where there is faith, is it not fair that man sleep with man and woman with woman? It is not the lusting, but the way in which we chose to lust that makes a mockery of love. We chose to force ourselves upon another, and then stand in judgment of our neighbors. Yet we dare not judge ourselves. It has always been thus.

"We have evolved from beasts and have been given a higher purpose: a mind with which to think, and the will to choose, but too often we choose to abandon our neighbors. We ignore the gift of compassion.

"Where is the greater good? Forever we let ourselves, our God, and his Son, down. We are all the same; fools. Faith is not to be kept behind walls or used for chattels, for if this is done, at what cost to the Son; at what cost to ourselves?"

John has been sitting near me while I've been typing, and I have asked his permission to edit some of what he has talked about. He is a powerful speaker. I could punctuate almost every passage with an exclamation mark, but that would make it difficult to read.

Before altering any of the trances, I have to ask permission. If I try to change a word and it alters the meaning, I feel sick. It feels like the worst episode of embarrassment I have ever experienced, but without the blushing. My limbs become heavy and begin to buzz.

John the Baptist is deeply distressed that the men who wrote the Bible had not shared their lives with Jesus, and yet it is the cornerstone of faith that directs many people worldwide. It's noteworthy that John and Itharus taught Jesus to write, and telling that none of his writings appear in the bible.

John believes in the power of leadership, but is disturbed by its corruption. He believes in leadership for guidance, not for dominance. He also supports the beauty of love and sex between both opposite and same-sex partners, but only in love and good intent. This opinion surprised me, not because I have ever been homophobic, but because his persona didn't encourage me to think he would voice this belief publicly.

John moves away from me, and the corner of the room dissolves. I see him walking across his beloved country, supported by a crock of sorts, and now I recognize him as someone who had visited me in my earlier meditations. With tears in his eyes, he turns and waves.

The spirits in my lounge room farewell John with a standing ovation, and I hear angels singing. This happens often, and although I don't recognize the words, I know they are singing. The language is foreign, but also familiar, and listening makes me feel as if I'm falling in love. Goosebumps rise on my neck and arms, and a feeling similar to vertigo overwhelms me. The tones are exquisite and when they end, a feeling similar to the satisfied peace after an orgasm stays with me.

JAMES FROM THE HOME OF ZEBEDEE

Immediately after I tranced John the Baptist, I tranced James. When I was coming out of the trance, I realized I had a different James in me than I thought. This was the first time this had happened. It unsettled me. It felt like waking from a deep sleep and finding someone you weren't expecting standing at the end of the bed, or the moment, while travelling to work on the train, you realize your pants are on inside out.

Unaware of the transition whereby John the Baptist left my body and James entered, when I came back, Gegu gave me the name James, but I thought of Jude and Jesus' brother James, not Zebedee and Miriam's son James.

James is standing beside me watching me type and apologizes for unsettling me. He is taller than I expected, has an Olympic swimmer's build, calm brown eyes and a tanned complexion. He's Calvin Klein sexy; a long haired cowboy wearing biblical fashion. He is a little reserved around me, but I believe I'm feeling the relationship he had with Judas.

James

"John the Baptist has spoken of the day he baptized us. He supported us with his arm, laid us back in the water and said the words he knew.

"'Please, God, welcome this young man with your grace; he is asking for your love and forgiveness so he may show it to others and heal with a truthful heart. He has come with your Son, who has come to save his people, and he has come to save himself."

"John the Baptist embraced me. You could feel he was overflowing with love, overflowing with strength, because he had lifted you into the arms of God. He was fifty-nine years old, and his grip was like iron. His dark eyes bored into you and made you feel he knew all about you.

"Many people had come to hear John the Baptist and Jesus speak. They lined the riverbanks. Jesus healed the sick, while my brother John and I shepherded the needy from the crowd.

"There was always tension in Zebedee when Jesus pulled us away from our fishing, but we were grown men and enjoyed getting away. We also enjoyed it when Jesus returned from his travels and shared the knowledge he had gained from the masters he had schooled with.

"He sat with people and saw places we never dreamed of; we had heard whispers, but we had no understanding of the wonders he shared with us. We looked at him with awe, and he filled us with the most glorious sense of well-being.

"Jesus had his dark moments too, but these he had in private. Like a shadow, he'd be standing beside us and then he would be gone. He'd leave us camped for the night and appear the next morning fresh and smiling. There was no arrogance with his passion, only a force that drove him. He was calm and gentle, but he could still inspire his people.

"I had seen him lay his hands on men bigger than him for things he believed in. When men took a stick or raised a hand against their wives and children, or against the beasts that served them, Jesus had the courage to stand up to them.

"I had watched this emotional boy grow up and had seen him throw many tantrums, whereupon his beautiful mother had always calmed him. Jesus knew of his father's unfaithfulness, and yet he never turned away from him. He knew from where his flesh had come, and he looked into his father's eyes with love.

"On another occasion when Jesus took us away from our fishing, we slept under the stars for three days and listened to him speak. He taught us the healing words, and soon the memory of those words will come back to you.

"The following year, we were introduced to Judas. I did not greet you warmly, but I accepted my brother's wish that you join us. You are not the same Judas this time, and you have a chance to redeem yourself. This is the lifetime in which you must free yourself. "

Briefly, I'm aware of my body and mind, and I realize my mind has been *watching* me speak. My mind is startled that this John is speaking. My body jumps as if electrocuted, and I feel embarrassed and alarmed that my mind may have influenced what John was saying. John, knowing this, reassures me.

"Relax, Simon. I see you are troubled, but you have not made a mistake my friend. God bless."

James was a lot more relaxed when we tranced again three days later.

James

"Simon, I will try not to unnerve you this time. I am James, son of Zebedee and Miriam, or so I thought, because I now know that my father was Joseph. When I heard this, I felt disorientated, a feeling I only experience when I come to you. I have been watching you work, waiting for another opportunity to speak with you.

"I was three years older than Jesus and did not have a lot to do with him until he was two. I tried to drag him to his feet, but he was a quiet child, and I soon lost interest in him.

"Zebedee had me on the sea in my sixth year. I took to it like a duck to water, for it was in my blood—ha, ha, or so it seemed, for it was not, really. Ha, ha.

"I spent a lot of time with my big brother Luke, who didn't have time for boyish games, but he taught me everything there was to know about fishing. Luke's whole life revolved around fishing and emulating our father. At home, he cared for our mother and his siblings. He was first mate of the household.

"He was not overly affectionate, but it was comforting to be with him. In my eighth year, he stood up for me and stared down a man three times his age. He was not one for fighting, because he did not need to. Everyone was cautious around Luke, and he was the one people turned to for advice.

"The family talked about Jesus and all the things he could do, but I did not notice his special ways until I was nine years old. The seas were rough, and there was no fishing, so I offered to take Jesus for a walk to get him out from under Mother Mary's feet.

"He was shy around me because we had not spent much time together. We walked through the market and down to the shore and looked over the fishing boats that had been beached. Then, with Jesus riding on my shoulders, we wandered away from the boats.

"We walked on and found a turtle, which was not uncommon, but rarely seen on the shore. I flipped it onto its back, wondering if I could drag it home, and was amused by its kicking legs.

"I turned to Jesus. He was in tears. I thought he was a foolish little boy. He ran at me, pushing me back, then turned the turtle over and led it back to the water. I'm not sure what happened next, but as I came to my feet again, ready to shove him back, something pushed me to the ground again. Sitting on the ground looking at Jesus, I realized all the fight had gone out of me.

"Jesus said, "I am sorry James. I didn't mean it." I tried to act tough, but it was all show. He had unsettled me. As we walked back home, he was quiet and reached for my hand. When I pulled away, he held on to my hand tightly, and in no time at all he had me smiling. He had that effect on me for the rest of my life. Whenever I saw him, he would make me smile.

"When Jesus was twelve, I found him sitting alone looking at his torn and bloodied hands. He had been working with stone with Joseph. I took pity on him and led him down to the water to bathe his hands and wipe his tears. "I'm trying so hard, but I seem so clumsy," he said.

"'Cheer up. In time your hands will harden," I told him, ruffling his hair. Leaning down so I could look into his beautiful blue eyes, I said, "Come on," and gave him a shoulder ride to a cove that was good for swimming. We swam and laughed together—just the two of us.

"Six months later, we met again and spent an afternoon together. We walked out of town and came across a shepherd bent over one of his flock. I didn't know what was wrong with the sheep, but Jesus grabbed my arm, pulled me toward the old man and said, "Wise old father, I can help you. I can save it." Then, he put one hand on the shepherd's sleeve and the other on the sheep, and a light appeared around them.

"Something, like the force that had held me to the ground when we found the turtle, stopped me in my tracks, and I could see someone standing behind Jesus. I didn't know who I was looking at, but I knew what I was feeling. I knew what love was, the love of youth where your tummy turns and your heart flutters. I had fallen in love; that was what I was feeling, watching Jesus.

"He stepped back, smiled and said, "There. Isn't she beautiful?" Then he hugged the old man and the sheep, looked at me and smiled, and ran past me. He asked me to race him back to the market, so I did, laughing all the way. He ran like the wind, laughing and smiling.

"Between fishing and his trips away, we did not see much of each other, but when we did, we had lots to talk about. I told him about working on the sea, the things I had seen, and the love I felt working with our family. Jesus also talked about the things he had seen, although I didn't know where—in heaven, perhaps. He was always excited, and every time he touched me he filled me with wonder.

"Jesus did not ask me to be a disciple. I felt compelled to go with him, and I was pleased when he pulled me away from fishing. I know it pained Zebedee, but he had other sons and many fishermen. My father was forgiving, but I know it worried him when I was with Jesus. As the years went by, I could see the reason for his concern, because the things we did provoked many people.

"Sometimes I protected Jesus from physical violence and cautioned those that jeered us, but Jesus' power came from the love and forgiveness he showed his people.

"His gift to his brothers was the knowledge he shared about the places he had been, the conversations he'd had with wise men, and the healing skills he taught us. We did not realize we could still do it without him, and when he was gone, it pained us—not because of the loss of the man we loved, but because of the loss of our faith."

"I thank you for the love you are sharing with us, and I am pleased with the words you are writing. God bless you, young man."

James's farewell and approval means more to me than I'd expected. I want to smile, but my lip starts quivering. I was unaware, until that moment, that I needed someone to be proud of my trances.

JESUS AND JOSEPH'S PASSING

We have put the children to bed early this evening, and Joanne I are enjoying dinner without them when Jesus joins us. I close my eyes and sigh, holding my breath for an instant until my heart pushes through the cocoon of stress that always seems to envelop it.

I feel Jesus' familiar vibration before I hear him say, "Hello." Joanne cannot hear him like I can, but her guide, Miriam, tells her he is here. Jesus kisses her cheek, and Joanne's eyes change color; darting golden rays turn her hazel eyes green, and the air around her shimmers. Joanne smiles.

Joanne only talks to Miriam, ignoring other spirits around her, but she reacts to the vibration of new spirits in the house, sometimes nervously. She knows when her father is near, she can smell him, and she'll talk about the conversations she has with him and his father.

Gegu, Miriam, Jesus, Joanne and I talk quietly so we don't disturb the kids. We don't talk about the book, work, or anything stressful. We talk about our dreams, and the funny things the kids have done. Miriam is standing behind Joanne, brushing her hair, Gegu is floating in the lotus position, looking every bit the Buddhist monk, and Jesus has pulled up a chair and is studying our meal—lamb chops, home-made fries, and salad. He turns to me, smiles, and indicates that he would like some.

I wonder if Joanne can feel what I can see. Does she know Miriam is brushing her hair? Her head is tilted to the side towards Miriam's brushing hands; she looks content, flushed, a little sexy.

Jesus is attentive to every gesture Joanne makes and listens to everything we talk about. His facial expressions change as if he's speaking out loud. It feels like a relaxed evening with good friends; just what Joanne and I needed. Jesus has sat down to dinner with us over the last few nights. He is pleasant company, and I have grown fond of his presence.

I had tranced while the kids were in the shower, so after I kiss Joanne goodnight, I sit at the computer and work with Jesus and Gegu.

Jesus

"Hello, my faithful Simon.

"I was ten years old when I first sat with John the Baptist, and he made me nervous. His eyes were black orbs, and he could hold me still with a single stare, but he taught me many things, and fuelled me with his fire and passion. We meditated and journeyed together—leaving our bodies we walked with angels, and we healed the sick and the unwilling. When we tired, Itharus fed us and made us laugh, and he knew when to caution John to let me sleep.

"Together, they talked to me about other people's beliefs, and they challenged me to think beyond my community. They taught me about the energy that can be harvested from the earth, and how to use this for God's work.

"History does not portray these men accurately. They did not preach from written word; they worked with men, from the heart, and this is how they instructed me. If I resisted, John the Baptist would grab me and shake me then look into my eyes and say, "You know your path, boy. I will die for you, so you must live for me." All his life, he had spoken of my coming, but he knew his fate as I knew mine.

"Up to the age of twelve, Itharus travelled to collect me for my lessons. I worked sparingly with my father, which fed his anger and caused tension at home. Mother Mary deflected his anger by feeding him, bathing him and lying with him. She made sacrifices so I could learn to control my power.

"Returning from a place beyond Egypt, where I had been studying with masters of meditation and secondary thought (*mastery of the unconscious mind; the duality of life and mindfulness*), I found Joseph frail and ill when I arrived home. Having foreseen his death, I had known for some months he was ill, but what shocked me was his wasting: his eyes were sunken, his skin pale, he had lost too much weight, and he walked with great pain. He was always a powerful man and a powerful speaker, but it amazed me still how someone so strong could become so weak.

"Mother Mary had tended to him for many months, and, although he was still able to walk, he was often confined to his bed. Joseph had not asked for intimacy with my mother for almost two years because he knew the sickness he had; that of sleeping with unclean women.

"She knew the reason, of course, but kept this from the family. No matter what he had done, he was my father, and Mother Mary's husband. I could have laid my hand on him and taken his sickness, but I would not, for it was the price he had to pay for his actions. How it tore at my heart, and how quickly I walked away from him. My mother's faith was strong, and she had my gift, but our world was not like yours, Simon; she was a mother and Joseph's wife.

"Come morning, while our family slept, I held my father's hand and we walked down to the shore to meet the sunrise. Joseph struggled to pass water. Afterwards, I supported him while he bathed in the cool sea, and then dried him in the morning sun. He was like a child, the tears running down his face. This was the first time he was truly able to meet my eye.

"He pleaded with me to heal him, pleaded with me to take his pain away, but I could not. However, I could take his shame, and this I wiped away so that he might have some peace. Before the fishermen who were returning from their night's fishing could disturb us, I led him back home.

"I kissed his eyes and cheeks and when I held him, I could feel his bones. Where was my strong father? I knew I could heal him, and it burdened me that I could not, but I did not cry in front of him, saving those tears for my journey. I bade my mother farewell and when I held her in my arms, I filled her with love for the days ahead.

"Joseph passed away three months after my departure, having lain in bed for many days. My mother bathed him, wiped the waste from his body, anointed him with oils and held his hand as she watched the life slip out of him, but she did not cry until he was gone. Even though I was not there, I carried the pain of knowing every detail. Not all men can be healed; many have a price to pay.

"While Mother Mary held his hand, Joseph begged her forgiveness, and she forgave him—she had always forgiven him. What wonder filled this woman? Mary was no virgin when she gave birth to me, but she was innocent, pure and strong. She knew who she was, the things that made her, where her emotions came from, the pain she might feel, and the loss she would endure.

"There was but one burden in her lifetime, and that was when she lay with Lazarus—but he needed her love and her comfort, and she needed to give him these things. It was a small thing in her life, and she found peace in this before her passing. She passed free of burden, of guilt and emotion. Her spirit was strong and pure—virginal."

"Joseph chose to stray, and it was his choice to burden himself with guilt. He had no acceptance of himself, which is why Hannah was sent to you. She was lustful, but it never overcame her, for she accepted it and did not burden herself with it. She shared her love, her goodness, and her smile and, unlike Joseph, she was not branded a harlot because she carried herself with honesty. She was true to herself.

"There are lessons for mankind in these stories; on faith, on life, and on love, and they lead to my Father. Use what is instinctive; look to the emotions in these lessons. You are wasting the ability of your instincts because reasoning is overcoming your physical selves, which is the vessel for your Fatherhood.

"My Father had asked Joseph to suffer, and this is why I was unable to heal him. I knew where he had contracted his disease. I knew the maiden's name and where to find her. I knew her suffering, and that I could heal her.

"This is my gift, and yet all who read these words have this gift. Am I not a man? Do I not have two eyes and two hands? Do I not look like you, walk on two feet, stand on two legs, and do I not breathe the same air as you? What is it that separates me from you? We are all my Father's children, and I am no more special than you.

"My family is like yours, and your neighbor's. The people were not perfect, and their stories were neither magnificent nor dull. They just *were*."

"I will share a story of my childhood friend Isaiah, a merchant's son, who came to our home occasionally. Together, we'd run and hide, and pretend that sticks and pieces of wood were spears and swords for our games.

"Isaiah did not see my healing gift. He only saw a boy living next door. Whenever we could, we'd play until dark then bid each other farewell and return to our families.

"I did not see Isaiah after his seventh year. He later became a politician of sorts. He wed, had beautiful children and lived a life of truth. He did not cheat or steal, and he tried to serve the people he loved and cared for. He cautioned the Romans, and their wrath descended on him. He was beaten many times, but again and again, he got to his feet to protect his family and his people.

"Is he any less special than me because he could not inspire, because he could not heal, or because he did not know God? I think not.

"You have chosen to worship the cross—a symbol of murder. Would you not be wiser to worship the hand of Isaiah, the hand with which he cradled his children, the hand he held up against the Romans, the hand he used for a kind gesture to his kin and his townsfolk?

"There should not be kings amongst men; only people with skills willing to share their knowledge. There should be understanding, and divine love, and a brotherhood of neighbors. Do not follow me; lead.

"We are all children, and we come from the same Father. History records people who have raised armies, and people who have stood against armies, but they are all just like Isaiah; they were once someone's friend, someone's childhood companion.

"Power corrupts your world and builds ego and greed. The Christ is not magnificent; it is Isaiah who is great. Wealth is not the corruptor, only the wealthy personality. So many people believe in the wealth of the one God, yet they draw arms against each other and draw blood in the name of the Christ, His son. Do not use my name. Stand in your own pride, and use your own name. The Christ is not the way.

"The Christ is the path to the wonder of God. My people, could I have shown you another way? Could I have shown you a better way? Each one of you is the Christ, even those in the darkness—but you are lost. Good Christians or good murderers, you are all lost."

Jesus left my body quickly, and listening to the tape, I could hear his frustration in my voice. In trance, I felt like standing and pacing restlessly. Jesus' moods shift quickly, but the most dominant emotion I can only describe as heartache.

He is the most passionate, driven man I have ever known, yet an aura of peace and love surrounds him. The mission he had undertaken, and the resistance and misunderstanding amongst his followers, tested the fortress of faith he had built.

His incredible gifts gave him a celebrity status he didn't want. His message was to look inward, find God, and then see this abundance in everyone and everything. The disciples followed, but no matter how often he encouraged them to do so, they failed to walk beside him.

Jesus was alone. He found sanctuary with the women in his family, and freedom in death.

How do we blend our flesh with our spirit so we do not travel on an emotional roller-coaster ride to disaster? The peace that resides within each of us seems to be as vulnerable as a fetus carried by a drug addict. Maybe this is what reincarnation is all about. We keep coming back to learn how to be children, to learn how to be carefree, to be innocent and honest, because this is how we are born. The trick is growing with innocence, and maintaining our purity.

"I know we all have the gifts of Jesus, but why is it so hard to access this gift?"

"It is as hard as you make it."

"Thank you, Gegu, but I do not understand."

"The path of no path, my son. What is it I am showing you?"

"Nothing?"

NOTHING

I'm excited, because I'm looking forward to telling Narelle what Moses and I talked about today. Tonight, the meditation circle is being held at my place, and Narelle has arrived with Anita, Sean and Stacey.

I start to feel uneasy when the four of them sit side-by-side facing Joanne and me across the dining room table, instead of sitting casually and haphazardly in the lounge. It looks like a military tribunal, and Narelle is the nominated spokesman.

There are no formalities. Narelle and the others state plainly that they believe I have been taken over by a demonic force, and that my trances are inaccurate. Narelle says she tested me and I failed, but she won't tell me how I had been tested. I only asked once.

It was a hard night for me, seated at the table facing four people I believed in, and whom I thought believed in me. Without interrupting, I listened to what they had to say. On reflection, I don't know why I didn't ask them to leave my home, but I think if I had, my disappointment would have turned to anger, and I would have said things I'd later regret.

According to the group, the *dark side* controlled me during my Biblical trances. When I tranced Narelle's deceased son and everyone's guides, I was the best trance medium Narelle had ever had the pleasure of working with. I didn't comment. I knew that she'd always need a more Godlier Jesus than the one who stood silently with Gegu.

Narelle assured me everyone was here tonight because they cared about me. That statement caused me to bite my lip and clench my fist. Gegu placed his hand on my shoulder, "Be still," and the love I had felt for them dissolved and was replaced with pain. They were concerned I had become a puppet for the lord of darkness, and had unleashed an army of dark angels that was now stalking them all.

Joanne said little, but she knew I was hurting. She waited for everyone to leave, then hugged me. She has always believed in me. Later, I lay awake for a long time, thinking and listening to Joanne's breathing.

I knew Gegu was close, but because I was still in shock, I was unable to hear him clearly. When I closed my eyes and asked him why, instead of seeing him, I saw a man who had appeared in many of my earlier meditations.

He's slimmer than Gegu. His well-worn robe is the color of cured sheepskin, and his eyes are dark orbs. His head is shaved, and his white beard, which grows only from his chin, is long and flowing. He appeared in the most unusual places: sitting cross-legged in the branches of a tree, perched on a rock ledge or on a log pendulum supported by heavy ropes which form a pyramid above him. He never spoke, and his face showed no emotion at all. He sat and watched me, and I assumed he was a guide, but I never had a name for him.

Hurt by the night's proceedings, I'm unable to sleep, and now my unnamed companion is sitting cross-legged and floating in the corner of my room. His beard and drooping moustache are being moved by the energy around him, and he emits golden light. Either he is a long way away, or he is only sixty centimeters tall when seated because he looks elf-sized against my wall.

I sleep periodically. Every time I open my eyes, my elf is still there. By morning, I'm hearing Gegu again, and I ask him who he is. "You know who he is, my son." Sometimes Gegu drives me crazy. This response, from that moment onwards, becomes his standard answer whenever I ask, who wishes to speak to me. I guess he thinks I'm old enough to ride my bike without training wheels.

My floating companion stretches his legs and walks into me. I spend the day looking through his eyes, which is like wearing gold-colored lenses. Everything is fuzzy and too bright. I can see auras on trees and amorphous waves of energy radiating from the ground. Watching birds fly is like watching bullets travelling in slow motion in a *Matrix* movie.

By the afternoon, I have solved the mystery of the floating man: he is who I would be if I were someone's guide. He is my higher self, and has no name, because he is *me*. He has been Gegu's guide when I have not been reborn to share a life with Gegu.

How do I know this? Because *I* told myself. I know, maybe I do need an exorcism, or at least a psychiatric evaluation, but my floating man arrived because I needed him. I needed my higher self so I wouldn't lose faith and abandon this project.

For days, I felt no spirits around me, although I knew Jesus and his family were still there. My higher self stayed with me until my faith was restored. He is like a blanket of energy around me, and he connects his energy to my own. Since he has come, I don't tire as quickly when I am trancing, my connection with Gegu is stronger, and I am hearing other spirits more clearly.

The miracle, I believe, is that I did not need to ask for my higher self to come. When I needed him the most, he arrived. All Gegu had been teaching me started to make sense. I began to get a *knowing* of the Universe, and I have more to look forward to.

Now, let me travel back in time to a conversation I had with Diane about soul groups. Diane's interpretation of a soul group is a group of spirits who descend to Earth together to live lives that influence each member of the group. A family's collective spirits could come from the same soul group, but the group also extends to people who become friends or partners through marriage and relationships, and includes people considered to be enemies.

Diane believes, and so do Narelle and Anita, that these spirits come down together to experience life through different combinations of relationships, then die and return again, and somehow this strengthens the spiritual energy of the group.

A lot of New Age literature and other spiritualists also support this principal, and I agree, although I don't know why or how. Gegu has told me not to limit my thinking; not to limit myself.

Mother Mary, Jesus and Gegu told me my spirit comes from the Archangel David. For a plumber that means; David is the keg of beer, my body is a schooner and I am—*the best a man can get*—beer.

Gegu helped me to understand this during meditation. I realized the vision I was seeing was symbolic, but I was still surprised. I'm hanging suspended, but I have no body. The only sense I have is sight: it feels like I'm turning my head to look, but because I have no head, it is only my *sight* that is moving.

In my vision, we are each cocooned inside a teardrop, amongst a mass of teardrops. We hang like a bunch of grapes with a larger gold, translucent, teardrop-shaped sheath supporting us. Looking around, I can see more bunches hanging from a golden vine. This vision extends as far as I can see. Individual vines are attached to a mother vine; like solar systems forming a galaxy. Each galaxy is connected with golden highways of light, which lead to a brighter source.

Teardrop-shaped grapes are falling from their hosts like dripping water, floating to Earth like golden rain and entering the Earth's atmosphere in an explosion of golden light.

I believe that when Jesus came to Earth, his entire galaxy of grapes was shaken from the vine by the hand of God, and Jesus' spirit plummeted to the Earth like a giant tear-shaped comet, supercharged with love.

The lesson was to realize individual spirits are connected to a higher source; there is no separation, because we are all from the same vine. Knowing this, I need to hop into Dr Who's phone box and travel forward to the morning of the day on which Narelle, Anita, Sean and Stacey nailed me to my dining room table.

It started much like any other day: I was unenthused about going to work, and as I drove away from home, I bid Gegu a sleepy good morning and asked how he was feeling. "I am well, my son, but I have a bit of a headache." This moment of levity started a day filled with discovery and enlightenment.

I had been thinking about the spirit of Jesus, about his soul group and about how many people on Earth, if any, have come from this group. Jesus has said that his spirit will not return to Earth again in its entirety, but he also said there were two people on Earth claiming to be him.

I thought about this as I worked: Jesus the man, my brother, is talking to me—not Christ, not God's Son. Moses joined us. We talked while I dug holes to connect downpipes to underground drainage pipes.

I started to think about God, and Moses reminded me of a *conversation-with-God* moment. This happened during the week I had tranced Moses, and I grasped there were two separate energies: Father God, who was forceful, passionate and made my body shake and vibrate in a rhythmical cadence, and Mother God, who was gentle, encouraging and took all the tension from my body, causing me to slump forward as if I was asleep.

I do not believe God entered my body, or that I spoke with God's voice, for Gegu showed me that He—which I now describe as consciousness, for I believe we have created the Christian God—connected himself to me with a silken, golden thread and used me to communicate. Father God introduced himself as "I am, I am," and, at the time, unbeknown to me, a similar phrase was used in the Bible when God spoke to Moses.

Narelle recognized the phrase, and Moses later confirmed that God had spoken to him using the phrase "I am, I am."

Seven years after I used this phrase, I researched its origin, and learned that scholars and theologians disagreed with the exact translation from the Bible. "I am that I am," "I am that I be," "I am He who is," "I am who I am," and "I am my name" are just some of the many translations.

Either way, these expressions meant nothing to me at the time I used "I am, I am" while trancing. I am no theologian, but it looks as though God has never actually said what He is. I am, I am … what? I asked Gegu. His reply surprised me.

"God is nothing."

"What? How can God be nothing? God is the Universe. God is everything in its entirety."

"Describe the Universe to me my son."

"Well … it's … it's indescribable."

"Then it is nothing."

"How can this be? God is the power that keeps us alive; He is the energy of our creation. The Universe is energy, and from that the Earth was formed, and evolution followed. All these things we have talked about."

"Where did this energy come from?"

"From God."

"Then what is God?"

"I … I … umm … don't know."

"But you do. You have been told. I am, I am. If He is not something, then he must be nothing."

Now Gegu and Moses are studying me intently. They are not making fun of me; they are waiting patiently, and suddenly, light materializes around me. My mind is racing, and then I ask the question, "Where is Jesus?"

"He is in you."

"In me? How can he be in me when we have spoken so many times about his soul group?" What was I missing? Who else has Jesus in them?"

"Whom do you wish?"

Now I'm really confused.

"Only because you wish to be," says Gegu, reading my mind.

These are the conversations I have with Gegu. Every spirit who comes to me calls him "the funny man", but to me he is "the exasperating man". This has made him smile, and he is watching me intently.

"Who is Jesus, my son?"

That's easy. "The Son of God."

"And who or what is God?"

I'm not going to let him catch me out again. I'll play his game, and stay one step ahead of him. I'll surprise him for a change.

"God is nothing, Gegu, and so that makes his Son nothing too, and if that is accurate, then I am nothing as well. No one comes from Jesus' soul group, because there is nothing to come from. We all come from the big fat nothing in the sky."

I think I'm being smart, but I've been led to the answer. I have asked many times about soul groups, if there is such a thing. And indeed there is: we are all energy—spirit—part of a higher energy source. This source is connected to a higher source again, and then again, and again, and these connections continue until the final connection, which we describe as God.

We are all part of Jesus' soul group. We must be, because we are all part of the Universe. We are all a part of God. You cannot describe God, but He has said, "I am, I am." For centuries, man has been trying to describe what He is. I think what God was trying to say was, "I am, I am, I am no one thing: I am nothing."

The original vision I had of soul groups disintegrated. There is only one soul group, and that is God. His voice guides us, and we are able to hear His voice because we have the ability to do so—we use language to communicate. Animals hear with their senses; they know where to search for water without knowing how, and they do not question how they know. Man always asks questions, and to ask a question is to look for something. Sometimes there is nothing to be found.

Gegu has been trying to get me on "the path of no path" ever since our first conversation. I cannot describe the rush I felt when I discovered *nothing*. Gegu and Moses are smiling, because this is what faith is all about: creating something out of nothing. Spirit is our connection to God, and the more we worry over it, the harder it is to connect.

From Jesus, I know he did not come to be the catalyst to start the Catholic faith. He had no intention to build churches or any house of worship. He did not want priests to spread His words. He did not want his Father's message translated in a book. He came as an example of how to live, how to love, and how to forgive.

He asked his disciples to follow His example. But I know, Judas knows, and Jude has told me, that as he gathered the twelve, some formed alliances, while others argued and looked for favor, and Jesus' example was misinterpreted.

God is not to blame for our children's deaths, nor is He to blame for the destruction of the Earth's ecosystems. We have taken the gift of creation and turned it to destruction; the destruction of all that is good here on Earth and the destruction of all that is good in man. We *created the darkness*, and spirit is trying to get us to clean up our own backyard before we destroy theirs. I guess we can start with *nothing*.

THE UNKNOWN SOLDIER

Night after night, I have been up until 2 AM. It is easier for me to concentrate and talk to spirit when my family is in bed. Gegu is helping me edit the manuscript, and at times I am looking over my shoulder reacting to the energy of interested spirits.

There is so much energy in my home that objects and ornaments are moving by themselves. The old hardwood frame of the house and the corrugated iron roof speak to one another as they cool, and their banter keeps me company, but the bumps, scrapes, and shuffling whispers of bodies moving makes me think about zombies. Nightly, during the months of trancing, a set of eighteen designer plates, standing on their edges in the kitchen turned around or to the side. This movement stopped when I finished trancing.

At 2 AM in a dark, quiet house I'm as jumpy as the next man, and if I become unsettled, I ask Gegu to move back the spirit I'm reacting to. There is nothing worse than the unknown, and if we can't see something, then we cannot determine how much of a threat it is.

Having finished typing for the night, I'm feeling edgy. I'm reacting to a new presence in the house. I feel like a hand is reaching for my shirt to pull me back, so I lean forward reflexively and scuttle to bed. I'm thankful for K-mart sales and the crisp security of one-thousand ply Egyptian cotton— good for wrapping mummies and strong enough to resist scratching zombie fingers.

The following morning I mention my unease to Joanne. She tells me she also felt agitated when she went to the toilet in the middle of the night, so much so she had turned a light on, only to feel that someone was watching her pee. While Joanne and I are having this conversation, someone apologizes for frightening her, and when I hear his voice, I know he is a Roman soldier.

Even with Gegu and Miriam's help, I am unable to hear his name. Later I speak to Max and Janu, but still his name eludes me.

I apologize to this brave young man for my unease, for I know he has only been trying to get my attention. This was an emotional trance, for grief had broken this young man. Everything good inside him had been erased by the passion and violence of war. He believed in something great, and this dream had been exposed by something greater—the love of a blue-eyed boy.

This is for every Unknown Soldier whose life was not taken in battle, but whose heart was broken by survival.

The Unknown Soldier

"I was sixteen when I killed my first man. It was easier than I expected, and I have since killed so many I've lost count, but I had always dreamed of being a soldier and fighting for Rome. I did not wish to be a farmer and till soil like my father.

"Rome was an empire that I thought was worthy of serving, but my service was murder. The things I have done, the things I have seen over the years—old men quartered, children beheaded, mothers and daughters raped and left on the ground like discarded pieces of clothing. Laughing, we left them there and did not think of them again.

"I had not returned to Rome, and my family, for twelve years. What had become of me? I gloried in battle, pitting myself against other men, cutting them down with a blade for the might of Rome, but I was no more than a rapist and murderer, taking from people who had nothing to give.

"There is no glory in collecting taxes; there is no glory in invading people's homes, the homes of good people, farmers like my father and mother. We were tyrants and driven by boredom. We soiled possessions and killed livestock, not even taking the meat, leaving the carcasses spoiling in the heat.

"What glory is there in beating children to the ground, standing over them and clubbing them for pieces of silver; silver that did not even make it back to Rome, silver lost in bribes and violence, silver that only fattened our centurions. And the maidens, the young maidens—how many did we rape? So many that we drank to help us forget, but come morning, we would do it all over again.

"We frequented Nazareth, and her people hated us. They were afraid. Their fear gave us power and made us brave. One time, we had a fruitless day. It was hot and dusty, and our tempers were frayed.

"We approached a family and stopped them just for looking at us. We beat the father, pushed the mother to ground, and handled her young daughter for our pleasure, while the seasoned veterans were already lifting their loincloths. As we dragged her away from her family, a small boy ran among us and wrenched his sister free.

"Looking at him, I saw myself reflected in his eyes. I saw what I had become. He stood beside his sister protecting her, and as we circled him, the people of Nazareth encircled us. A comrade grabbed the boy and punched him to the ground, while the girl retreated and found safety in the crowd.

"The boy was beaten and kicked, then bludgeoned with the flat edge of a blade. As I watched the life flow from him, I do not know what possessed me, but I charged my fellow soldiers, driving them off the boy. When we grappled, the centurion rode amongst us, trampling the boy and knocking me over.

"Rising to my feet, I struck out at the horse, forcing the centurion back, and stood over the boy with my sword drawn. All the violence I had seen gave me the courage to stand against my comrades, and I swung my sword, cleaving an arm and opening a face.

"The crowd found courage and stood against my fellow soldiers. I continued to stand over the boy while my former comrades retreated. Dropping my blade, I looked down at the boy, and picked up his lifeless body. I held him in my arms while the crowd stared at me with hate-filled eyes.

"Falling to my knees, I held the boy's body to mine. I didn't know I could feel so much pain, and I cried tears for all those I had sinned against. A boy's blood was on my hands, and in my heart were the cries of every maiden raped and every innocent slain.

"I looked up, and a child was standing in front of me: a child with the strangest blue eyes. He reached out and laid his hand on my forehead. I cannot describe what I felt, but suddenly the lifeless child in my arms began to stir.

"All around us was silence—peace—for my comrades had retreated and left me for the mob. The child in my arms came to life. His mother pushed through the crowd and took him from me, and I was left kneeling in disbelief on the blood-soaked ground. The blue-eyed boy was still standing in front of me. "You must forgive yourself. You must go back to your farm and family, and you must not take up arms against your fellow man." Then he held out his hand. I placed my hand in his, and he lifted me to my feet. I was twice his size, yet he overpowered me, and he overpowered the mob.

"He asked me to take off my breastplate. I obeyed. I stood only in my loincloth, but I did not cry, for I felt as though a weight had been lifted from me. I never took a drink from that day on, for I never needed to forget.

"It took me many months to reach my home, and when I did, I found that it had been burnt to the ground. My family's bodies lay where they had fallen. The livestock was gone, and the wells were poisoned; this was the price you paid for desertion. The glorious empire for which I had fought for so long was now ash at my feet. I laid my family in the ground then wandered over the land I had called home, but at night when I slept, I dreamt of a boy with the most beautiful blue eyes.

"Thank you for listening to me."

By the time the soldier had returned home, his family's bodies were well decomposed and had been picked at by vermin and wild dogs. It was difficult looking out of his eyes and standing in the scorched shell of his home. I took a long time to recover from this trance, and my healing guide draped a blanket around my shoulders and sat with me.

The soldier is standing silently beside me as I type his trance, and I ask him if he is all right. I hear a faint "No", but he does not wait to be comforted. He steps away and walks slowly through the ruins of his home once more.

Jesus

"The Romans did not come to Nazareth often, but it was enough that they came once every three or four months. The people of Nazareth were good people and did not deserve to lose their silver to the taxes of Rome. Violence did not always accompany these visits because the Romans knew they were outnumbered, but when violence did occur, it was invariably swift and brutal.

"The Romans preyed upon young girls and mothers, and the men who were responsible were tainted with death. They did not ask for pleasure; they took it.

"Many soldiers were slaves who had been captured in battle, then forced to serve Rome or die. Violence was freedom to many, for war was what fed their starving bellies, and rape became what fed their hearts. Man is a creature of habit, and the habits of Rome were to conquer and overcome lesser people.

"I was nine years old when I saved the child and the soldier. I was doing my chores when I felt compelled to leave them and go to the market. Nearing the market, I heard the sound of raised voices and saw a crowd gathering around some Romans who were holding raised swords and lances.

"When I hesitated, Ellucshion pushed me forward and a small boy walked beside me, the spirit of the one who had been beaten. I held his hand and led him through the crowd. In amongst all the pushing and shoving, a pathway opened, and I seemingly floated towards the kneeling soldier. It was as if my feet were not on the ground, simply walking above it.

"When I placed my hand on the soldier's forehead, the boy's spirit returned to his body. I know Ellueshion shielded the soldier from the crowd while I talked to him and helped him to his feet, but how this was possible I did not know then. I felt the soldier's anguish, and I could see his life unfolding in my mind. I saw his future, and it was his future path of loneliness that broke my connection with him. While the crowd jostled me, the soldier fled.

"I do not know how the crowd overlooked me, but there were many times when people could not see me; this was just the first. Even I did not know the full power of Ellueshion; she is my Father's miracle.

"I walked home shaken and perplexed and returned to my chores. I saw the boy I had brought to life many times after that, but he did not know me. Soon I would be distracted by my teachings with Itharus and John the Baptist and would also have to work with Joseph, and this event faded from my memory.

"Once again, I thank you, Simon. Walk with God."

SARAH AND THE ANGEL CELESTE

When Sarah (not James's wife) first spoke to me, I was working with Max. She told me she was Jesus' friend, and she was so familiar that I asked her if I knew her. She smiled, and as soon as she did, I knew she was the archangel Celeste from the valley.

Celeste's smile has been infused with rainbows and the breath-holding excitement of watching whales breach. She doesn't need Botox or Photoshop to make her lips more desirable.

I tranced Sarah on December 29, 2000, while I was away with Joanne over the Christmas break. This was an unusual trance, because when Jesus spoke, he was in my body with Sarah. I don't know how this is possible, but I trust Gegu. This wasn't the first time this had happened, but it was the most beautiful.

Sarah

"My name is Sarah. I was six years old when I met Jesus for the first time. From my family's home, I could see him sitting on the beach looking out to sea. He was twenty-four years old, and he was beautiful. When I approached him, I saw tears on his cheeks, but he made no sound as he cried. I walked up, stood in front of him and reached for his hand. "What is it that bothers you, Jesus?" At first he did not reply, so I continued. "I am Sarah. Why do you cry?"

"'I am alone; with all that I have, I am alone.'"

"'But you are not alone. I am standing here.' I smiled at him, and he smiled back. 'I will be your friend.'"

"I sat with him and chatted, as six year old girls will chat, about anything and everything. He did not say much, so I held my hands out to him and pulled him to his feet. We walked hand in hand along the beach, while I carried on with my light banter. When it became late, my mother called out for me, and I said; 'I must go, but if you would like, I will play with you tomorrow.'"

"I didn't see him again until I was twelve. He was sitting in the same spot, so I ran down to the beach and saw that once again, he was crying. 'Hello, Jesus. Why are you crying?' I asked him.

"'Because I have no love. I have a child, a son I cannot come home to at night. I have many followers, people who look up to me, and there are others who fear me. They destroy our land and look at me with evil in their eyes. I only want to come home and sit at a table with a wife and a son.'"

"'I am but a girl, but today, I can be your son. Today, you can speak to me of the places I have heard that you have been. Today, you can share every happy moment with me; all the excitement and joy,'"

"I pulled him to his feet and led him to the water's edge, and then I asked him questions while we walked together with our feet in the water. Climbing onto his back, I made him carry me. We continued to talk until the sun dipped down below the horizon. My young brother came to find me, and I said to Jesus, 'I must go. Today I was your son, and this is a memory you can hold dear. I am your friend, and perhaps I can talk to you again tomorrow.'"

"I did not see him again until I was sixteen, however. He was thirty-four years old, and this was the year of his death. He was sitting in the same spot. This time he was not crying, but he looked weary. He smiled when he saw me, and said, 'I knew you would come; you have always come when I sit here. Are you an angel child?'"

"Looking at him, I replied, "Does it really matter what I am? I am your friend; I am Sarah. I have looked for you every day, and now I have found you three times. Twice, I have relieved your burden. Twice, I have lightened your heart. What can I do for you today?"

"'This is the last time I will see you. This is the last time I will sit here. All I was sent for has come to pass, and will it not bear fruit?"

"'You are the fruit; you are the fruit that nourishes our people," I said, gazing upon him.

"'I have many followers, and yet I look to you. I have my Father above, whom I have carried, but who will carry me?"

"'I, Sarah, will carry you. I will carry you because you are my friend."

"'I have no wife to mourn my passing, and my son does not know me."

"'Today I will be your wife. We will walk along the beach, look out to sea and find your son fishing, and we will speak of the gifts he will bring you."

"We walked hand-in-hand, and I leaned against him and said, "Jesus, you have been a good man. You have been a good husband, and you have fathered many sons. The land that we walk upon is the home of your sons. They will walk here for many years, for many generations to come, and no matter what will come to pass, I will be your friend, your son, and I will be your wife. I am Sarah."

"Then Jesus embraced me and cried. We sat quietly together into the evening and watched the stars come out. I knew who he was: he was the Son of God. He was but a child, however, and I was his friend.

"You know who I am, Simon. I am Celeste, and as the girl Sarah, I eased a beautiful man's pain. Did he accomplish nothing? People have forgotten him and who he was; people have forgotten what is inside him and only see him on the cross. The Jesus I knew was not on the cross. He was beside me; his tears fell on me, and I strengthened him so he could meet his destiny. His destiny is not yet fulfilled, because you have kept him on the cross, all of you—all of you who read these words."

When Max and I talk about Jesus, we know he didn't burden anyone with the things that worried him. He was a private person and hesitated to ask for comfort. As John and Judas, we assumed he could cope with everything; he was invincible, and we believed in him, for he was the Son of God. Leadership is a lonely role because people expect you to be strong, but Jesus didn't come to lead; we elevated him to that position because of what he was capable of doing.

The sad thing for Max and me is we feel we should have known when Jesus needed our support. Jesus gave so much to the people around him, but those people didn't think to give anything back. I only wish I had asked if he was all right more often, and, when he couldn't answer, that I had hugged him more.

God placed Sarah in his son's path. Jesus knew this as he showed us with his question, "Are you an angel child?"

THE BROTHERS LUKE AND MICHAEL

Luke and Michael are the first and second-born, respectively, of Zebedee and Miriam. Luke has been waiting patiently for his turn to speak. He's a giant like his father, with light-brown wavy hair and silver-blue eyes which look like sunlight reflecting off the sea.

Luke is a powerful man who walks through his hips, gliding like a dancer. He has a muscular, balanced physique, and his presence commands respect; he is a leader of men.

Luke inherited Zebedee's house after Zebedee and Miriam moved to Capernaum. He became head of his family and ran his father's fishing fleet. He married a local Nazareth girl, Catherine, and had twelve children with her.

Luke makes me feel confident and in control when he enters my body. When spirits are talking about a childhood memory, I find I adopt the mannerisms and emotions of the age they are sharing, so I think Luke was born strong and confident, because this is all I am feeling. I know there is a part of him that is gentle and caring, because I can feel it, but he exudes confidence.

Luke

"I loved my father from birth, and my eyes always followed him, begging for his attention. When I started walking, my mother would say,

"Walking right out of the house," because I loved to go down to the beach to swim.

"My father first took me out on the water when I was three years old. I loved his company, and the sound of his voice, and even though I had only been walking for a little while, I already had my sea legs. I loved the feel of the spray on my skin, and the smell of the sea, but most of all I loved being with my father, listening to his voice and looking at his smile.

"He was different on the sea—a force of nature—and I wished to be just like him. At four years of age, I was fishing with him. He'd let me hold the tiller, although it controlled me more than I controlled it. I did not realize he had tied it in place, and was proud that I was helping him.

"By age six, I was helping him to pull in the nets, and by age nine I was able to do it by myself, my father standing beside me, encouraging me.

"I spent every waking moment with my father, and I wished to be at his side always. At fifteen, I was big for my age and had been on the sea for many years. My hands were hardened, and I was strong.

"I stood by my father and my family and cared for my mother. I loved her softness, her smell and the feel of her hands, and whenever she'd let me, I'd brush her hair. I got as much pleasure from this as from being on the sea.

"For many years, I overlooked Jesus, even though I had been over to see the new baby on his return. One day, I looked across and noticed him clinging to Mother Mary. He was six years old, and he looked unhappy, so I offered to take him for a walk.

"This was the first time I had spent any length of time with him, and we walked through Nazareth and out into the desert, looking for flowers for my mother, because this made her happy.

"While we were searching, we came across a feeble old man lying in some shade. I tried to hurry Jesus past him, but he would not budge. Looking up at me, he said, "Please, Luke, don't leave him lying here.""

"'He is but an old beggar, a smelly old man, and he is here because he has no family," I said. "His family has turned away from him, and it is not for us to care for this old man."

"But Jesus was insistent. He looked up at me again, placed his hand in mine, and stared into my eyes. "Please, Luke. We cannot leave him here. He will die. He is one of us."

"Jesus touched my heart, and softened me, and when I looked into his eyes, I noticed they had changed color, like the sea. Resigning myself, I went to the old man, who smelled worse than the animals, and Jesus touched me again and said, "It's okay Luke," and suddenly I could smell the old man no more. Now, there was only the fragrance of flowers, but unlike any I had smelt before.

"Jesus ran in front, looking back over his shoulder and beckoning me forward while I carried the old man to the sea. We found a sheltered spot where I stripped off his old rags, and together we bathed him. As we did so, his skin started to glow, his eyes sparkled, and he smiled. Then, Jesus touched the sores on his body, and they disappeared.

"I didn't question what I was seeing, but I question it now. Laying the old man in the sun, I washed his clothes while Jesus sat and talked with him. Shaking my head, I wondered what I was doing.

"I laid the now clean clothes in the sun to dry then turned and looked at Jesus and the old man—who didn't look like an old man any more. He looked young, and alive, and his shame and sadness affected me. He had been living with his daughter and son-in-law, and when his daughter died, he had been put out onto the streets to scavenge and beg.

"I walked along the beach to clear my head while Jesus continued to sit and talk with him. While I was thinking, his clothes were drying in the sun, but I had no idea what I was going to do with him. I wandered back and helped him to dress, and noticed he had regained some of his strength, although I still needed to support him and help him walk as we led him home. We must have been a funny looking trio; a giant supporting a skinny old man, the pair being led by a laughing, skipping boy.

"When we arrived home, I asked my mother for some bread so I could feed him, at least once. She looked amused, but didn't say a word, nor did my father, who had watched us walk to the door. Jesus kissed them both then wandered off home. We shared a meal with the old man, and gave him two loaves of bread, some goat's milk, and a blanket.

"'Thank you. Thank you for your kindness," he said. "Today, I thought I would die. Then someone came to me and said; "Wait, a child comes; he will touch you, and he will give you the will to live." I cannot remember my day; I can only remember sitting at this table. I am ashamed that I cannot remember how I arrived here, and I cannot pay for your hospitality; I can only thank you with my heart." With that, he departed, and we never saw him again.

"My mother, who was sitting opposite my father, placed her hand on my shoulder, while my father said nothing as I looked into his eyes. "Something happened today, Papa, something I cannot explain to you. Who is Jesus, Papa? What is he? He frightens me so, yet he fills me with wonder."

"My father said nothing, merely shook his head. Then I thought I heard him say Michael's name—Michael having been lost at sea. Before I could question him, however, he was gone. My mother hugged me and said, "You are a sweet boy. Come and help me with supper."

"This is the only story I have to share with you about Jesus, but in one day, he filled me with love. When he was taken to his death, I was on the sea, where I have spent my whole life, and of all the wonders I have seen there, the strength and commitment of men to work for their families, and the love I have received from my father and mother, nothing compares with the love I experienced that day with Jesus.

"I thank you for your service to my family."

Luke left smoothly, and Michael slipped in; one exhaled breath and it was done. Michael has been with me from the beginning of this book, but he has a soft vibration, and I hadn't noticed him. Gegu assures me that he has been observing all this time, and if Luke had not introduced him to me, I believe we would not have tranced.

Michael never married, but instead lived with Luke and his family. However, he found a partner when he was forty-seven years old, an Egyptian slave girl, Patrika, whom he rescued from execution. She bore horrific scars from years of torture, and she had been condemned to die for breaking her master's neck.

People were afraid of Michael. It was a superstitious time, and Michael's demeanor unsettled many, so no one raised arms against him when he untied the girl from the executioner's block.

As I write, I see these scenes unfolding. The girl is stretched across what looks like an old stump. She is kneeling, and is tied to the stump at her hips and thighs. Her arms are stretched out in front of her, also tied; a position that exposes her neck for the executioner. Michael walks through the crowd and gently pushes the executioner aside. The executioner starts to raise his curved sword, but Michael turns and looks him in the eye. Suddenly, all the tension drains from him, and the crowd is silenced. Without a word, Michael unties the girl and carries her off through the crowd.

When I ask why, Gegu replies, "Because he was able to." Michael is a mystery, and answers like this from Gegu make him more so.

Michael and Patrika had no children, but helped raise Luke's offspring. After Luke passed, Michael waited for three days, during which he ate and drank nothing. He then kissed his scarred love one last time and wandered off. His body was never recovered, and he left all of his fortune to his Patrika.

Many things have surprised me as I have journeyed to this book's completion, but not even Jesus has made me feel as calm as Michael, who is standing beside me now. He's a titan, and I can sense his hidden power, yet he is so still. Normally when I trance a big man, my body feels like it is under pressure trying to fit the person inside me, but Michael only served to straighten my posture: I felt alert but peaceful at the same time.

Michael described himself as the village idiot, but Gegu would not let me say that. Gegu was helping Michael with his words during the trance. At times I felt like I was speaking, but the note-taker was only recording selectively.

I don't like to use the words "simple" or "slow" to describe Michael, but this is how he seems. He's different, that's all, and for all his strength, he feels like he is still a boy.

When I'm looking through Michael's eyes, it feels like I'm seeing for the first time. His mind is so still that all we focus on is the scene before us, and all my senses are heightened. "Breathing in the essence" is a term I could use to describe his every action. When Michael said, "I particularly loved spending time with Mother Mary," I assumed that they did chores together, or sat and talked, but what I was seeing was Michael standing close to her whenever the family came together for meals and functions. As big as he was, I don't think Mary even noticed him. Michael enjoyed the rise and fall of her chest, the changing tones of her laughter, the tilt of her head, and her delicate scent.

The only emotion Michael feels is love, but in varying degrees. When he describes being teased by other boys, I still only feel love. He is Luke's faithful shadow, and although Luke is Michael's protector, there is a memory stirring of a time when Michael defended Luke, but it is of so little importance to Michael that, even though I can *feel* it, I cannot put it into words.

Michael is incapable of being surprised. He knows no fear and is not afraid of pain or death. He sees spirit clearly, for this is his world. The spirits who walked with him to the cave to sit with Jesus were wise men and sages: Moses, Noah, and Abraham were in the group, as well as holy men from other Eastern cultures.

Michael didn't understand the spoken language of these men, but he connected with their faith, love and calmness. We battle our minds to connect with spirit, but Michael's mind was always peaceful. He was not dumb or slow, just calm. He seems to be a very private man and economical with his speech and actions. The conversation he had with Jesus in the cave was the biggest speech he ever made.

He's standing close to me, and I am tingling all over, humming. He has just spoken to me.

"I have to go."

"Why?"

"I must. Thank you."

Then he is gone, and I ask Gegu what he has to do. "He serves God, my son. He has always served God."

"Is he an angel?"

"Yes. He is *the* angel. He is the one who watches over Jesus; the one who watches over all of God's children."

"I do not understand."

"Some things, you will not. Soon, my son, soon."

Michael

"I am Michael, brother to Luke, son of Zebedee. Luke is two years my senior, and he is more than my brother; he is my friend. He has stood by me and protected me many times from the teasing of other boys in the community, and I lived with him until he died.

"I said little and kept to myself. I was not a great fisherman like Luke, but I fished to serve my father. Some called me slow, but those that did answered to Luke. Though I was taller than he, I was softer, and I'd often end up in my mother's arms after all the teasing, for I did not wish to raise a hand against another. I was happy doing what was asked of me, and I loved being with my family. Spending time with Mother Mary is something I particularly loved.

"I was quiet and friendly and liked the company of both my family and myself. There was a place I would go, a place that was special to me: a cave. I found it by chance when I was eight years old, and I had to crawl inside because the opening was so small.

"People thought I took no notice of anything, but I took notice of Jesus. When I looked at him, I could see a glow around him, and I could see many people following him that no one else could see, but I said nothing. I did not speak of this to anyone; even though I heard the words he heard and saw the things that others could not explain.

"When Jesus was still a child, I'd watched him come home with his little treasures. He knew where I slept, which cot was mine, and often I'd find a gift there; a butterfly or a shiny stone. We'd never spoken, but I looked across at him, and he looked back at me, and I knew where his gifts came from.

"One day, when I was sixteen and he was nine, I approached him shyly and asked him to come with me.

Smiling, he looked at me and said, "I have been waiting for you." I had no reply. I walked ahead, and he had to run to keep up with me.

"I took a winding path to my secret place. Together we crawled into the cave and sat. There was a crack in the rocks, and when the sun was in the right position it lit up the crystals hidden in this place like twinkling stars. We sat together, and Jesus put his hand in mine and said, "Michael, look what I can do." Suddenly all the crystals came to life and began to sparkle. It was as if we were sitting in front of a fire of rainbow-colored flames.

"We were not alone, for others were now sitting with us, and I heard the words they spoke, but I was not a good speaker. I was not surprised by what I was seeing in the crystals, for Jesus did not surprise me. We sat for hours in silence, listening to the voices around us.

"When we left the cave, we took the direct route home, walking hand-in-hand. I did not say goodbye when he went to his home and I went to mine. Afterwards, I went out fishing and did not return for two days, but when I did, I found some desert flowers and pretty stones on my cot.

"Unlike my brother, I know who Jesus is. Jesus is the Angel of Peace. He is the angel that touches each of us when we sleep, so nightmares will not come.

"In the year of Jesus' death, I woke one night and walked to my cave, accompanied by men unseen by others. Many of these men had lost their lives for faith, and many spoke words I could not understand. I listened, but I am not a good speaker. As I neared the cave, I saw a glow coming from the entrance. I had not visited this place in many years, but I knew who was inside.

"I crawled in and sat with Jesus. He said nothing but turned and smiled and put his hand in mine. All the crystals were glowing brightly. I looked at Jesus. Tears were on his cheeks. As each tear fell, the crystals grew dimmer. Eventually, there were only a few crystals still shining, and he said to me, "What does it mean?" People rarely asked me questions, but this one I could answer.

"'Sixty days from now, a light brighter than all of us—a light that we cannot see because it blinds us with its brilliance—will fade, and then we shall see it, and we shall see what we have done. And those who are there on this day will carry it for the rest of their lives. They shall carry it for their lives to come, and they shall not look upon an angel without fearing it. I shall not be there for your passing, but "I" will be there."

"Jesus responded with his acceptance. "This, I must choose." We sat together until dawn, then walked home. We met Luke on the beach. Jesus embraced us both and said to us, "You are strong, like your father, and you are wise, like your mother." Then he took Luke's hand. "The family is resting upon your shoulders. You are the one who will watch over them."

Then he embraced me and said, "You are the one who will stand by your brother," and then he was gone. I did not see him again.

"I thank you for letting me use your words, because without you I would have sat here in silence. I hear, although I am not a good listener, but I have listened to you; I have listened to you type the words of my family, and soon it will be done

"You are not aware of the angels who stand with you, for you have only just begun, but I can see them; I can see them."

Michael is an angel.

For me, this trance with Michael and Jesus had an ethereal quality to it, even more so than the spirit rescues with David. The world of spirit was visible, overlaid on top of Michael and Jesus' world. The crystal cave felt unearthly. Increasingly, I'm having experiences in my life where periods of time and angelic, other-world beings, are visible and interactive. I wondered if the crystal cave was *real*.

I cannot stop thinking about Michael. The phrase from Gegu, "the angel", has been niggling at me. Gegu has told me that Michael's spirit rests in another boy in South America. Once again, he's a gentle giant, a member of a large, poor family, and brother to a boy with Jesus' spirit. Why that boy? Why that location?

Gegu doesn't answer me, but I'm guessing there's an opportunity for the boy to become a great leader. Jesus' spirit is in all of us, but why aren't angels in every family?

Who is Michael? I know that he is more than an angel; he is the power that protects us, the father of all our children, the light in our world. I feel foolish when I speak like this and imagine myself standing at an intersection wearing a sandwich board proclaiming Armageddon—*repent sinners, the end is nigh!*

Michael's standing with Gegu, watching me work and flooding the room with smoky, golden light. He's curious to see how I unravel the mystery of Michael. His calmness is what it is like for an angel to be in the flesh, and his giant frame is what was needed to control his energy.

If God is the captain of the good ship Earth, then Michael is the first mate, and, like all good first mates, Michael knows everything about the running of his ship. Jesus' life was a pivotal moment in the earth's history. His life has influenced billions of lives, and I feel that Michael's angelic presence was needed for Jesus to reach his full potential. Michael smiles and dips his head.

All angels are spirits, but not all spirits are angels. There are various levels of energy and knowledge in the realm of spirit. Spirit is energy that manifests as angels, guides, other worlds, healing, foresight, instinct, and, I am sure, a lot of other things I couldn't explain.

Spirit does not judge us, no matter which path we choose to tread. Our guides are here to guide us. They will not lead, and are supported by what I call travelers: guides who will teach a specific skill, or open a pathway on our spiritual hard drives so we can absorb information, but are not any individual's guide per se.

Even though spirits never judge us, there appears to be a balancing process—a cycle of progressive experiences in the realm of spirit, and we keep returning to the Earth until our spirits have experienced every emotion. Why? I don't know.

Gegu is saying, "You know, my son," but I am floundering. Gegu and Michael are not disappointed with my reasoning; I'm the one who is struggling.

"The path of no path, my son. What is it I'm showing you?"

Nothing. And it is here that I will understand who, or what, Michael is.

JUDE AND LOUISE

On the evening of January 14, 2001, Joanne and I went for a barbeque with her family. As I was speaking to Joanne's sister about her guides, her daughter sat beside me and said hello. At the same time, Jude greeted me with his usual cheeky smile. I asked him what he was doing here, but before he answered, I knew: he was my niece's main guide, and she had been Jude's cousin, Louise.

After Luke and Michael, I tranced Jude. These were all comfortable trances for me. My trances have become easier since my higher self has come. They are not so physically draining, and my throat no longer gets sore.

Although I have seen many sides to Jude, all of which are endearing, he has never shown me such longing, and in spite of his entirely relaxed manner, his love for Louise was a heavy load to carry. He has just said, "I carried it gladly." Jude has been waiting patiently to share this story with me, and now he has the chance.

During the trance I am sighing and swallowing from the emotion. Jude's longing is a physical force pressing down on my body. My chest feels tight, and Jude's anguish at not being able to marry Louise can be detected in my voice when I listen to the tape.

Jude

"I'm eleven years older than Louise. On the day she was born, I visited Miriam's home and asked if I could see the baby, and I loved her from that moment. I watched her grow. When I was not away working with my father, I'd take her for walks and talk to her.

"She had a beautiful singing voice. Oh how she could sing, and when she sang, I loved her even more. How I longed to marry her, but I could not for she was like a sister to me, and my family would have turned away from me."

Jude sighs, and I feel like I'm in love.

"She'd bring all her secrets to me. Whenever Miriam reprimanded her, gently of course, she'd come to me with her crocodile tears. She came to me with the story of the first boy she had kissed, and I longed for it to have been me, and then the first boy she lay with, and again, I wanted it to have been me.

"One night, when I was twenty-six and she was fifteen, we walked together. She was a beautiful woman. No matter how long she worked on the nets, or how many fish she cured, her hands always remained soft and her skin unblemished.

"This night, she leaned against me and said, "There is a man I wish to marry. What should I do, Jude?" Well, my heart broke. She was leaning against me, warm and soft, and here was my chance to tell her how much I loved her. Instead, I pulled her closer and asked, "Do you love him?"

"'I think I do,' she replied, 'but if I marry him, he will take me from you.'

"Many things were arranged in our time, and Louise's marriage plans met with approval, so she married him in her sixteenth year. At the wedding, I danced with her and threw her into the air. We laughed and smiled, and kissing her cheeks, I wished her well, but how I loved her. I have loved her all my life, and never married because I loved her so much.

"When I was sixty-seven years old she returned, widowed and childless … was there not hope for us now? We lived side by side in the former home of Luke and Michael, alone. Slowly, cautiously, we came to lie together.

"Luke and Michael now lived together in the home of Zebedee, who had long since passed, and so, surrounded by the bustle of Luke's children and grandchildren, our union was blessed.

"I lived a long life, Simon; ninety-six years, and before it was over, my love was taken from me once again. In my eighty-second year, my Louise passed. She lay in my arms and I listened to her last breath leave her, and held her until her body was cold. We had no children, but the years we spent together had been most precious to me.

"So many did not know, Simon. They did not know of the love we shared, and now you can share it with everyone. I have waited two thousand years, but finally, I can shout it out.

"Yes, you know where I am now. My spirit has not returned to Earth. I am the guide for the one who was Louise, and I will wait, and when she passes into spirit again, we will come back to Earth together, and everything will be perfect. I will gladly give up all my memories of her to woo her and love her. We will have many children, but for now, I watch over her spirit and guide the young girl. This is what we have chosen, but soon we will be warm in each other's arms again."

It is January 16, 2001, and Jude has been watching me type his story. He is relaxed and smiling, and although he has shed a few tears, he has braved it through. He always makes me laugh; he has just asked for a beer. Gegu is floating in the lotus position, and Jude is leaning against him: Luke Skywalker resting against Yoda. I feel like they are laughing at me, and then I hear, "His typing hasn't improved, has it, big man?" Yes, thank you very much.

Jude is showing me his death. It's a glorious day, and Luke's grandchildren have carried his favorite chair onto the beach. Luke has already passed, and now one of his granddaughters holds Jude's hand and leads him to the chair.

Jude is sitting in the sun with his eyes closed, thinking of Louise and listening to the children playing on the beach. Now, Jude is talking to me, so I will let him finish.

Jude

"There was to be a wedding, and I was happy. I closed my eyes and listened to the joyful voices around me, but soon fell asleep. I dreamed about Louise; it all seemed so real. I could hear her and smell her skin. When I opened my eyes and stood up, there she was, smiling beautifully. It was a good dream; we held hands and walked to the water's edge. She told me she missed me and dreamed of me every night. I smiled and kissed her. I looked down at myself: I was young again, and Louise looked to be fifteen.

"We danced together the way we used to, and she started to sing, which made me cry. Then, she said, "Come on, I have a surprise for you." She danced ahead of me, out over the water, and I followed her, guided by her hair. We stood together on the waves. Turning to look back at the beach, I saw an old man sitting with his eyes closed. He was smiling, and his favorite chair was rocking gently.

"I turned back to Louise and saw that Jesus was now standing with her. The two people I loved the most were with me. Louise held my hand and smiled, and Jesus said, "It is time. It is time to stop dreaming because this is real. I have missed you.'"

No one is laughing any more, and I am crying again. They are all here; Jude, Louise and Jesus. Reliving Jude's death, the feeling of going into the light, overwhelms me. The emotion is too intense, the love painful, and the longing to return to the light causes my body to shake uncontrollably.

"Gegu?"

"I am here, my son. I am always here."

"Why am I always crying?"

"Because you care for them, my son. They all love you. I love you."

Louise

"As a child, I loved attention from Jude. I loved his smell, and he was never too busy for me, but I never thought of marrying him. I thought he only looked at me as his favorite cousin, but we were close. Not all my tears were crocodile tears, and he always knew what to say. He always held me just right, and I loved his sense of humor and his funny laugh.

"I thought love was grand and magical, and I looked forward to marriage and raising a family. I failed to recognize the contentment I shared with Jude was a love worthy of marriage, and for that, I am sorry.

"I fell in love with a handsome man but was happy for only a short period of time. He could not make me laugh and demanded much from me after we married. We were unable to have children, for I had many miscarriages, and my husband started to drink to ease his disappointment in me.

"Our relationship deteriorated, and he became fat and lazy. He was eight years older than me and eventually died from gout. I was not sad to see him go, for he had drunk and gambled away our fortune, and I was tired of serving him and his friends. It was a loveless marriage. I longed for Nazareth.

"Jesus guided me back home to Jude. He visited my dreams and told me Jude loved me still. He said that this was the man for me and that I must return to Nazareth.

"We had so few good years together, and I longed to share a perfect life with him. He filled me with so much desire, and in time, when he could do so no more, he filled me with love. He could always make me laugh, too.

"Pneumonia eventually took my life, and I watched him hold my lifeless body through the night after I passed. He did not burden himself with grief, but released me to heaven. He did not need to visit my grave, for he knew where I was; I was in his heart, where I had always been.

"He has come down to guide my spirit through this life, and there will come a time when you must introduce him to his young charge. He holds you in the highest respect. There is something in you, Simon, which you did not find in Judas. Jesus saw it, and I see it now; in time, always in time.

"I have only one story about Jesus. He danced with me at my wedding. As we danced, I happened to look up, and, for a second, his eyes changed color from blue to black. Reflected in them were lots of children. It was only for a second, and then he smiled and twirled me around. After the dance he whispered, "It is the future." Then I was whisked away from him to dance with another. He waved as we parted, and his eyes were blue.

"He always used to make me smile, and I loved him because he loved Jude, but what he was showing me was the life I would soon lead with Jude. It was my wedding, however, and I was young and happy, so I quickly forgot what I had seen.

Thank you for taking the time to listen to me."

Jude and Louise wave goodbye and fade away, and my lounge room looks like a room again. The life Jesus had shown Louise in his eyes was the life Jude is waiting for. For more than two thousand years, she has waited to live the perfect life with the man she has loved more than any other, and she has one more lifetime to live before she is in Jude's arms once again.

It makes our lives, and our deaths, seem all too insignificant. If you have lost a loved one, keep the thought close to your heart that soon you will be reunited. You do not have to take your own life to join them, for they have never left; they are just waiting for tomorrow.

THE FIRST ENDING

It's difficult to end something that has waited two thousand years to be recorded, but I am exhausted. Spirits, wanting to talk about the years leading up to Jesus' crucifixion, have visited, but I chose to start with his childhood, and Jesus has honored my decision.

It's hard closing the door on all the spirits who want to speak, and if I have been chosen for this, I hope I have proven myself worthy. It saddens me that Judas killed himself, but it's what joins me to Jesus; we both didn't need to die. God didn't want His Sons to die.

Jesus and members of his family knew he was going to die because they were mystics. Similarly, when Jesus visited his family after his death, they saw him because they were gifted. They needed him; we all need him.

This is what has eluded me. "He didn't need to die, did he Gegu?"

"No, my son. He needed to live." We killed him—humanity killed him—and then the disciples made a martyr of him, and Jesus became the excuse, rather than the reason, for everything that followed.

Jesus was sad because of the things he knew, while Judas was sad because of the things he had endured as a child, and this is what brought us together. I betrayed someone I loved.

On January 28, 2001, Jesus joins me for dinner. He smiles and watches me negotiating with my son, trying to get him to eat his dinner. I have asked him how he would like to close this chapter of his life, and he gently replies,

"Any way you wish." His blue eyes look into mine, and I can feel tears forming. He has always trusted me; it was difficult being the betrayer.

Dinner is over, and Joanne is covering schoolbooks for Lee while the children are playing in the shower. Ben Harper is singing *Waiting on an Angel*, and I'm sitting there sipping a XXXX beer, wearing a Wallabies rugby union jumper and thongs. To get any more Australian than that I'd have to change the CD to Jimmy Barnes singing *Khe Sanh*. It all looks normal, except there is a man typing slowly on a keypad while talking with Jesus—I really need to cry.

Jesus and I are listening to Joanne trying to get the children out of the shower when he says, "You are lucky. I wish I had what you have."

Do we really know how wonderful it is to be alive? I am not a wealthy man, but I am surrounded with wealth. My family and life's challenges nurture me. I don't know what's around the corner, and when I ask spirit, I cannot hear an answer—isn't that the funniest thing?

Can you imagine knowing what tomorrow brings? Would you really want to know? Where is the surprise in that? If we cannot be surprised, how will we evolve? Jesus' life was controlled by his gift, while around him, his family evolved. Whether their stories were good or bad, happy or sad, hopeless or hopeful—they were their stories, and it's not for us to judge.

Jesus lived his life through the people around him. He lived his life for all of us. It's a shame that history has twisted his message.

"Hello, Jesus."

"Hello, Simon. I have enjoyed your company, and I always enjoy your music."

"I love you, Jesus. I'm sorry I never told you more often."

"It is a small thing. You have always loved me, and you have suffered many lifetimes for this moment. We chose this together. I needed you to cry, so my family could share their emotions with you.

"My life cannot be put into chapters; it does not belong on pages. It belongs where it has always been; in the people I came to serve. I was born amongst the people Moses had saved, but this was only because they needed saving. My message was for everyone, for all my Father's children.

"I have loved all my family from the day I was born, and every moment with them was precious to me. I came to Earth to share the wonder of my Father, but it was my family who made my life wondrous.

"There was a time in my life when my mind was clear, and my path was set. I knew what had to be done, and that soon I would travel and learn with other masters, but what was missing from my life was love.

"The other young men of my age had maidens to be with, beautiful young girls of our people, but I was shy; for all that I had, I was always so shy. There was a young girl I was attracted to, Jessica, but whenever I would walk past her home, all I could feel was sadness.

"When I saw her in the yard, I'd admire her long black hair and beautiful dark eyes, and she would smile shyly and look down at the ground. For all my gifts, I did not see the obvious; Jessica was blind, which is why she never looked at my face. I was attracted to her sadness, drawn to her like a moth to a flame.

"Finally, I found the courage to say hello to her, and it was on this day I realized she was blind, for I startled her when I spoke. She was so beautiful and had an enchanting voice. I said, "Hello, my name is Jesus,"

She replied, "I know it is, young sir. I know who you are. I have noticed you walking by."

"What she was noticing, I do not know, but I reached for her and brushed the hair from her face. When she didn't pull away, I asked that she be healed, but she was not, and I wondered why. I visited her often after that. I'd be walking past and I'd ask to sit with her and we'd talk, but I could never get her to leave the yard.

"I had heard the story of the fisherman who had lost his wife, and now drank too much, but harmed no one, or so we all thought. But sadly that was not true.

"The fisherman's wife had died giving birth to twins. They had become entangled, and she had suffered for many days. On the day of her death, Thomas, the fisherman, eased his misery with wine, and would not let his friends and neighbors tend to the body of his wife.

"For three days he sat beside his wife's corpse drinking until Jessica, who was eight years old, approached him and pleaded, "Papa, I'm hungry." No one knows what possessed Thomas, but he lashed out at her, and continued to beat her, now enraged. His anger not yet sated, he then beat her younger brother until he had beaten one child blind and the other senseless. I had not heard this story before, and it did not come from Jessica's lips … I just knew.

"I invited Jessica to walk with me, but she kept refusing. She had become a captive in her home; a slave for her drunken father and a servant to his bed. Being her brother's protector, she could not leave. She was also too ashamed to cry for help. This is why I could not heal her, why I was unable to restore her sight; she believed she was not worthy of being healed.

"For two weeks, I sat with her, holding her hand and talking. For those two weeks I loved her, burdened by the things I knew, and that she did not have the courage to tell me.

"Then, one day I came to sit with her, and she was not there. A story is told of a maiden who swam out to sea and never returned. Why did she do it? She had been brutalized for many years: at first her father drank to overcome his grief, then he drank to forget the beating he had given to Jessica and her brother, and then he drank to steel himself to take his own daughter to bed.

"Was it the kindness I showed her, or the love she felt for me? Was it any of these that had given her the courage to swim to her death? I don't know. How did she know it was me who was walking past when, for so many years, I had overlooked her?

"I was at a crossroads in my life, and I called on my Father to avenge my Jessica. When next Thomas put to sea, a storm rose up and he was not seen again. Were my prayers answered? Is this where my power would lead me?

"You are now at a crossroads, Simon, and you cannot ask it of our Father, because he will hear you. You must steel yourself for what is to come.

"This is not the last time we will speak. This is not the last time I will use your voice. When you have rested, we will begin again.

"To all those people who will read your words, I say, find the goodness that is in your hearts, and when you have found it, you will find me, and then you will find my Father. You are not alone in this world. You have never been alone.

"I do not wish to be on a cross any longer. I wish to be a man. I wish to walk amongst the people I came to save. I wish for you to see me, because I am you. I wish for you to become me, because you already are.

"Walk in peace, walk in love, walk with God. God bless you, my faithful Simon, God bless you."

This is not the end; this is a beginning. Let us remember, lest we forget: "I do not wish to be on a cross any longer. I wish to be a man."

If Jesus had been alive this century and had been tortured and shot during ethnic cleansing would we hang a golden Kalashnikov around our necks and from our rear view mirrors? If he had been gassed in Auschwitz would bronze swastikas reach for heaven above our churches? How about if he was butchered with a machete during the genocide in Rwanda?

If he is someone's son then he has been in all those places.

THE FINAL WORD

It is February 1, 2001, and it is raining. This is how I began this journey—driving with Jesus in the rain. It has been a journey of enlightenment and self-belief, and Jesus and his family have travelled with me. They are watching me struggle with my typing, for I can feel them, curious to see what I will write next.

If I ask Gegu how many more spirits are waiting to speak to me, he smiles and says, "There are many, my son." Jesus and his family fill me with love, and I can feel the energy from the storm. Each drop has enough energy to heal a child. Competing with the golden mist that is radiating from them, the hair stands up on my forearms. Whose eyes am I looking through?

David is at my side. He moves into my body briefly, and I know what he wants. Somewhere in the Universe, we must once again battle with his brother. The man-beasts are rocking gently back and forth, drumming the ground rhythmically with their lances in time with the beating drums of the ancients. David is gentle tonight and touches my shoulder with his hand. His love almost makes me cry.

The only thing real is the computer screen and keypad. Everywhere I look, there is a sea of spirits, and everyone is watching me. All the children have gathered around, waiting expectantly, and I know who they're waiting for. She is the one who has helped me with my journey, who is joined to me by the love I have for Joanne. She is the Earth Mother, Miriam, and I have offered her the final word.

Miriam

"For many years, a man has been painted in shades of grey, but he does not need this camouflage any longer. Each one of us has the heart of this man, but so few of us know where to look to find it.

"My people were overcome by the sickness of false missionaries and poisoned by the diseases and temptations of God-fearing men. But which God did they serve? It was not the Father of the golden child. I watched my people, clothed and sated by God's missionaries, die with their buffalo.

"You have corrupted the words of God to suit your greed and ambition. You do not understand the earth that feeds you, and you have neglected the wisdom of Earth people. We lived in harmony with the earth, and the white man's sickness was unknown to us.

"The land of my ancestors has been overrun by the war cry, "For God and country!" This is not the God who sent his Son to teach His children, and my land, the land of my ancestors, has no place in a country ravaged by greed.

"For two thousand years the Christ, the golden child, has lain dormant in you, and I am shamed, for you are my children, I am your ancestor, and the Christ is your brother.

"Have you no respect that you are unable to believe His message? He is your brother, as He is my son, and we are His children. It is too late for the buffalo, but is it too late for us?"

"Thank you, Miriam."

She leans towards me and kisses me softly. When she embraces me, I can smell her musky scent, and we sway gently to the music emanating from the spirits at our back. They all come to their feet, and Jesus places his hand on my shoulder and squeezes it comfortingly. I can hear singing, and I begin to cry. I am always crying. Why am I always crying?

"I love you, Simon."

"I love you, too."

HOME

It is October 2, 2007, and Gegu is waiting patiently for me to find the courage to continue. It has been difficult to revisit Judas' memories. The archive is locked and chained with titanium links of guilt. My fingers pause, suspended in nowhere time, motionless above the keypad. My youngest son is eating a vegemite sandwich and talking to our dog, while a crow is distracting me with its repetitive call … I'm afraid.

"Of what, my son?"

"Of knowing what I have done."

My life is forever changed. I live between worlds; I am chosen. Jesus is standing with Gegu and smiles reassuringly. The energy of his smile connects us, and the sound of water bubbling from the aquarium filter takes me into the past.

Jesus is camped for the night with the disciples John, Paul, Mathew and Judas—yes, I am there. I've woken before dawn after a restless night, having slept with the memory of Jesus' touch. He had served lamb soup, seasoned with watercress, and fresh-baked bread. Before eating, he had carried a bowl of water to each disciple and washed our hands gently, compassionately; it has become his common deed.

I have stirred at every sound during the night, expecting the temple guards to loom out of the star-bright night at any minute. Now, it is almost dawn. Not being able to lie any longer, I am leaning against an olive tree listening to the soothing melody of moving water.

Suddenly, Jesus is with me. He knows he has startled me and places his hands on my shoulders. Staring into my eyes, he leans forward and embraces me. "It is time. You must go; I will not be able to save you. Forgive yourself: you must forgive yourself."

The words echo for two thousand years until Gegu repeats them to me.

Chills run up my spine and my legs start shaking. A horse snorts, and the sound of leather breastplates rising and falling in time with running feet disturbs the stillness of the cool morning. Jesus pulls me toward him, and I can see the sadness in his eyes. Then, he spins me around and pushes me away. "Run, brother, run!"

Propelled forward, I stumble and fall, rolling and raising my arms defensively, responding to the sound of a blade being drawn. The shadow of a body looms over me, and I am smothered by its weight. I struggle to free myself. Then I realize it is Jesus who is lying motionless on top of me.

Fingers grasp my hair and pull me away. The flat edge of a blade crashes into my hip. A knee is driven into my groin, and a forearm crushes my throat. In a nightmare, I can smell garlic and sweat. Abruptly everything is black.

My eyes slowly open, and my tongue feels swollen. The oppressive heat of the midday sun has brought me back from the sanctuary of unconsciousness. One arm is twisted beneath me, and my hip is numb. The memory of Jesus' face flashes through my mind like a lightning strike. The blood that has closed my eyes is his. I scream out his name, but the sound I make is no more than a rasping cough.

I stand unsteadily. The pain of the blood flow returning to my limbs is as painful as the weight of my guilt. Now I'm retching, and bile burns my throat and hangs from my chin. Jesus is going to die. I am responsible.

Images of Mary Magdalene and young Mark storm through my mind; I've taken from them the one who loves them the most. Walking gingerly, I'm confused. My tears turn to the sticky consistency of dried blood, as I remember the way Mother Mary looked at her son, and how she showed me kindness. I don't want to think anymore … I don't want to live.

The sun, heavier than my heart, falls towards the horizon. A twisted trunk, leaning almost horizontally, clings precariously to the bank on which I'm sitting, the bleached trunk and roots clawing at the parched ground. A braided length of leather is tied around the trunk, and my thumb caresses the oil-stained braids. Where did I find it? How did I get here?

I look at my left hand. It takes a while to comprehend that I can see dried blood. My eyes lift lazily and look across the dry watercourse. The sun is low enough that I can look directly into its golden orb. "Run, brother, run!" I don't feel anything anymore.

I've moved so quickly that the leather tied around my neck almost decapitates me. My legs flail in the air momentarily until I crash into the dust. My legs are twitching as if I'm still running. My bladder lets go and urine soaks through my clothes and into the parched earth, while the fingers of one hand twitch as if reaching out.

It's not over, not yet. Meditating with Gegu, I approach the body of Judas, gravel crunching underfoot. It's bright, and the sunlight makes me squint. A dragonfly buzzes past, and dust I have kicked up with my foot rises languidly in the heat. Is it real? Gegu is not here.

The weight of something I am carrying causes me to look down at my hand, and—magically—I find I'm holding a curved knife. Judas' body is discolored, and flies are busy crawling and laying eggs, while maggots of varying sizes are busy feeding. Ignoring everything, I gently cut the leather from around his neck and cut his robes away from his body.

Soft cloth and a gourd of water have now materialized so I straighten Judas' limbs and gently bathe him. Slowly, the flies and maggots disappear, the earth is washed clean of body fluids, and grass begins to grow while I am washing his face. He looks peaceful.

Sitting on the grass, I cradle his head in my lap and with the comb that has now replaced the knife, brush his beard and comb his hair. Looking up, I see the dry watercourse is now full of desert flowers, and white cotton sheets lie beside me.

Sighing, I lay Judas on a sheet and place his hands together on his chest. Leaning forward, I kiss his forehead and tell him I love him—and I mean it. Blossom petals begin to fall like spring rain, and a hand is placed on my shoulder. Turning, I find Mother Mary looking into my eyes.

"I'll take him home. His brother is waiting."

ACKNOWLEDGEMENTS

Gratitude owed to: Joanne for falling in love with me and raising our children; YA author, Natalie C Parker, for her generosity and wisdom; the editors, Hilary Smith (formerly THE INTERN), Jennifer Pooley, and fellow Australian and fantasy author, Dionne Lister for craft and vision—I couldn't have done it without you. Dionne, Aussie, Aussie, Aussie; Robert Baird for the perfect cover; Maree, for believing in me and my dream; Julia, for loving me and my children; Gegu, for always being there, and Jesus, for forgiveness and brotherhood. I love you all.

ABOUT THE AUTHOR

Simon, previously a plumber, has given up his love of pipes and trenches and is now a healer and medium; although he can still be coaxed into changing the tap washers at home.

Simon travels throughout Australia, and the world, undertaking healings and connecting people to spirit. Consistently, amazing health responses occur during healings. He's considered an expert in energy healing and has retired from karate. His abs disappeared, but his sense of humor is resilient.

Jesus and family still visit. When Simon is not out of his body he can be found playing darts and pool with his partner and family. He enjoys camping, watching movies, discovering new authors, and scares easily—a trait family and friends exploit. Dogs and old ladies still like him—it's a mystery.

Discover more about his amazing life and work here: http://www.simonhay.com/

Made in the USA
Middletown, DE
17 January 2016